◄ I ►
CHOSE
PRISON

▼

◄I► CHOSE PRISON ▼

BY JAMES V. BENNETT

Edited by Rodney Campbell

Alfred A. Knopf   New York   1970

CONTENTS

ILLUSTRATIONS

◄ I ►
CHOSE
PRISON
▼

IN PURSUIT
OF THE RULE
OF LAW

On a dark, windswept evening in Washington, two policemen patrolled the pathway leading from the Capitol to the Supreme Court Building, revolvers and walkie-talkie radios at their belts, K-9 corps police dogs straining at their leashes. That day at the Supreme Court, a five to four majority of the justices had ruled in favor of an accused suspect against those who insisted the court was showing undue leniency toward offenders. The head of the Supreme Court police assured the justices as they left for home that the women employees working late typing the opinions, making out the docket entries, would be escorted to their cars or the nearest buses. Not long before, a secretary had been assaulted on Capitol Hill on her way home, and a researcher for Senator Frank Carlson of Kansas had been murdered in her apartment a few blocks from the Senate Office Building.

The policemen and their dogs formed part of a special tactical force ordered to Capitol Hill by Washington's chief of police to make sure that no further harm befell the men and women at the heart of the administration of justice. Nationwide, according to the Federal Bureau of Investigation, there was a forcible rape every twenty-three minutes, a robbery every four and a half minutes, an aggravated assault every two and a half minutes, an auto theft every minute, and a burglary every twenty-seven seconds, and the chief of police was determined to fence the rising crime rate off Capitol Hill.

What a strange scene this was, and how characteristic of our times, I thought, as I strolled from the Capitol to my office and chatted with the policemen in the shadow of the Supreme Court Building, which so aptly expresses in its integrity of line the rule of law in our national life. The famous carving on the building proclaimed: EQUAL JUSTICE UNDER LAW. For twenty-seven years as director of the federal prison service I had served these words and now, in retirement, I was forced to face up to the question whether law enforcement in our country was a failure. The Presidential Commission on Law Enforcement and the Administration of Justice had recently reported that the spread of crime, the talk about crime, and the fear of crime were beginning to erode the quality of our national purposes. Specifically, said the commission, more than one third of the American public considered it unsafe to walk alone anywhere at night, more than one third kept firearms in their homes for self-defense, more than one in five wanted to move out of their neighborhoods because of the prevailing lawlessness.

"EQUAL JUSTICE UNDER LAW"—a slogan or a verity?

What kind of justice? I had so often asked myself, as I presided along with the police, the courts, the parole officers and my fellow prison officials over its uneasy administration. Was justice, as Plato felt, the harmony of the whole organism of society rather than the weighing of scales of strength and power among the different parts? Was justice an absolute in its true nature, which somehow changed its signature in the course of man's evolutionary concepts? What was the significance of justice to the criminal, to the victim, to law enforcement officers such as ourselves? What was its meaning to the men in prison—with whom I chose to spend the greater part of my life? They sometimes tended to think of justice in a bitter context: it was merely the sum of the machinations of those who had taken away their liberty. Other men in prison viewed justice as the lifeline along which they progressed in an orderly, humane manner to a future they might be able to cope with more efficiently.

Equal justice under law is now in danger of submersion, however, in the simpler, more savage shout of law and order. There is an uproar about the rising crime rate and a resurgence of the argument that offenders must be treated severely. There is plenty of reason. Since 1958, the crime rate has increased at more than five times the rate of growth of the population, and the increase is accelerating. Since 1960, crimes of violence have increased by twenty-five per cent and crimes against property by thirty-six per cent. The President's Commission on Law Enforcement says further that most crimes are not reported, that there are three burglaries for every one made known to the police, and more than seventy cases of employee theft—"white collar crime"—for every one brought to trial.

The rising crime rate is rooted, perhaps, in the undisguisable strain of violence in our national character. Our homicide rates exceed those of Germany and Japan, for example, by three to one, and surpass the murder rate in England and Wales, by seven to one.

I am, I realize, asking a great deal when I suggest that my readers take a cool, objective, and unemotional look at the crime crisis. This is not easy to do when "law and order" is one of the most important and most emotionally charged domestic issues facing this generation. Law and order has a different meaning to different people. To some, it is a mask for vigilante-ism—a cry for police-state practices, which divide our people with their overtones of racial hatred. To others, and I hope to most, it means a massive effort to prevent crime, assure personal security and guarantee freedom from fear by methods that will be fair, just, effective, and achievable in our lifetime.

Just how bad is the situation? There has never been a time when crime was not a major problem. It depends on one's point of view whether the days of Al Capone, the Tenderloin, Club-ber Williams, or Gyp the Blood were better or worse than those of the Mafia dope peddlers.

In the good old days there were no statistics by which we could measure crime with any degree of accuracy. Now we can do somewhat better, although our statistics still leave much to be desired. Moreover, there *is* a vast amount of unreported crime, as the President's Commission said, including burglaries, assaults, fraud, sex crimes, shoplifting, abortions (a single sur-geon said he had personally performed thirty thousand abor-tions in his lifetime), and so on. Most crimes are not reported to the police because they are considered private affairs, or the victims fear reprisals or say the police will do nothing. Often we talk about a vast increase in a type of crime that did not exist in the past or has lately been created. Automobile theft is a good illustration. More than 550,000 automobiles were stolen in this country in 1968. In 1930, the base year used by many for the measurement of crime trends, fewer than 200,000 cars were stolen. Automobile theft continues to grow at about the same rate cars are manufactured. But it is now included with murder, rape, robbery, and assault among the serious crimes that swell the over-all FBI crime index, which is going up at the rate of about thirty-five per cent per year.

It comes as a surprise to many people that crimes of violence —murder, rape, aggravated assault—have not increased nearly as rapidly as property crimes. Homicide, for instance, is about the same as it was a generation ago—5.1 to 5.6 per 100,000 of the population per year. The homicide rate is much higher in the South than in the North. It is eleven times as great in Alabama and Mississippi as in Wisconsin, Vermont, or Utah. Five, six or even ten times as many Negroes are murdered as whites, not only in the South but in the northern states as well.

Burglaries, purse snatchings, larceny, and simple assaults have tripled since 1940. While the homicide rate has remained stable, the rates of robbery, aggravated assault, rape, and other crimes have increased over-all perhaps fifty per cent above the low point of 1940. The rate has increased twenty-five per cent to thirty per cent more from 1960 to 1968. Therefore, the statistics must be read and interpreted with care. Everyone agrees, however, that crime is burgeoning and must be fought.

The principal victims of crimes of violence are the disadvantaged groups in our society, the urban poor, white as well as black. The highest rates of assault and robbery are found in inner cities. The National Commission on Civil Disorders reported that one low-income Negro district in Chicago had thirty-five times as many serious crimes against the person as did a nearby high-income white district of similar size—despite the fact that the low-income area had three times as many policemen per hundred thousand of the population as the high-income white area.

There is a significant amount of crime that cannot be prevented even by saturating an area with police or national guardsmen. Many serious crimes occur in homes, in shops, in youth pads, which are not accessible to the police. In approximately six out of ten cases of murder, rape, and sex crimes in a recent year, the victim knew the perpetrator. For nine months after the civil disorders in Wilmington, Delaware, in the spring of 1968, national guardsmen patrolled the streets, but they were not able to reduce the incidence of crime. Excluding automobiles, only ten per cent of stolen property is ever recovered. In these categories, the sad truth of our society is that crime *does* pay.

This is not to be construed as downgrading the importance

of an adequate number of policemen, properly paid and well trained. It is to suggest we do not accept the simplistic solution that putting a policeman on every corner will stop crime. We forfeited, for instance, two hundred million dollars in a recent year by embezzlement—about five times as much as we lost by bank holdups. No policeman could stop that.

Washington, D.C., which is now regarded by some as the crime capital of the world, has more policemen per thousand people than any other city of comparable size in the United States. Most large cities have about two policemen per thousand of the population. Washington has four. This partially accounts for the fact that Washington stands sixteenth among metropolitan areas in the United States in recorded crime. This is far below Los Angeles and New York City. Washington is not the crime capital at all, even though bank holdups have doubled between November 1967 and November 1968, and even though groups of Negro dope addicts have been shown on television proclaiming they will steal, even kill, to get money for their habit.

The escalation of the crime rate unquestionably reflects the scandalous stimulation of the mass media. One month to the day following the assassination of Senator Robert F. Kennedy, the National Association for Better Broadcasting began a week-long survey of programs televised by seven VHF stations in Los Angeles. In 143 hours, the monitors tabulated 452 homicides and 390 attempted murders. Television is guilty of selling violence for fun.

It is incredible that there is no federal gun registration and owner-licensing law on the statute books—this despite assassinations, governmental debates, presidential appeals, mass protests and the incidence, in 1967 alone, of 7,700 murders with guns, 71,000 robberies with guns, and 55,000 assaults with guns. In 1968 the country took a long step forward by banning mail order sale and shipment of rifles and shotguns and requiring the licensing of arms dealers. But when it comes to registration, the federal government and most of the states have not been able to overcome the pressures of organized gun owners whose unreasoning fears blind them to the imperatives of firearms control.

The rising crime rate is also intertwined with rising racial tensions. Four times as many Negroes are arrested as whites for major crimes, and ten times as many Negroes are arrested for murder. These immense differences do not testify to any inherent criminality among Negroes, however, because there is no difference in the rate of arrests among the Negro and white middle classes. Southern Negro farmers are among our most law-abiding citizens. President Lyndon B. Johnson was correct when he pointed out, "We must drain away the swampy breeding place of crime. You know where it is—in the slums of this nation."

The tragic riot in Newark, New Jersey, in the summer of 1967 was heralded by the crime statistics. Newark was first among all American cities in homicide, rape, robbery, aggravated assault, burglary, larceny, and auto theft, and it was a wonder that the blowup was so long coming.

Federal Bureau of Investigation Director J. Edgar Hoover strikes a popular note when he says: "There is too much concern on the part of the courts for the rights of an individual charged with a crime. I think he is entitled to his civil rights. But I think the citizens of this country ought to be able to walk all of the streets of this country without being mugged, robbed or raped. In my opinion, the courts in some instances have been entirely too lenient in the sentences imposed."

Chief Justice Earl Warren, striving for perspective, replied just as sharply: "We note today a tendency to blame the rulings of the courts for the vast amount of crime. Thinking persons and especially lawyers know this is not the fact. They know that crime is inseparably connected with factors such as poverty, degradation, sordid social conditions, the weakening of home ties, low standards of law enforcement and the lack of education."

At levels further down, the debate rages passionately among the professionals. The police state flatly that the courts are handcuffing them. But the courts accuse the police of attempting to circumvent their rulings on individual rights. The prison officers must sometimes bang their heads on their own prison walls to gain public attention. They find themselves regarded, increasingly, as merely the keepers of the people society wants out of the way. Some prison officers, fortunately a minority, welcome that role, among them Arkansans.

GUARDS SHOOT 24 INMATES, read the headline of an Associated Press story from Cummins Prison Farm, Arkansas, October 14, 1968.

> Prison guards wounded 24 convicts today when they fired blasts of bird shot into a crowd of penned-up prisoners to force them to go to work in the prison's farm fields.
>
> Superintendent Victor C. Urban said the use of shotgun blasts was a reasonable tactic under the circumstances.
>
> About 100 prisoners had refused to work until the prison authorities complied with several demands they had made. No convict had any type of weapon, Urban said. During the morning about 22 of the prisoners changed their minds and went to work. The remaining 75 or so were in a fenced enclosure when they were shot at.
>
> Urban said the first shot was fired by Gary Haydis, an associate superintendent. "Mr. Haydis told them to go back to work and they refused," Urban said. "He fired his shotgun in the air as a warning shot and they did not move. So he fired into them. Then they moved." Other guards followed Haydis' lead.
>
> "Let me make one thing clear," Urban said. "No inmate is going to tell Mr. Haydis or I or the prison board that we should run the prison this way or that."

The United States today has the largest prison system in the world, federal, state and local lockups, and I hasten to add that Cummins Prison Farm is scarcely typical, even though it does show how far we still have to travel before we can view ourselves as a modern nation. Every day more than 1,250,000 of our citizens are paying their debts to society in prisons, reformatories, work camps, work-release programs, training schools, and clinics, or they are under parole or probationary care. Every year more than 2,500,000 people are admitted to this vast "corrections" population, and their care costs us an incredible one billion dollars per year. Even more incredible, only one fifth of that fortune is earmarked for rehabilitation programs.

Society appears unable to plan the progress of correction, because it makes conflicting and contradictory demands. Society expects men to be punished severely for their crimes, so that others will be deterred from committing them. Yet society also wants men to be rehabilitated while in prison, so they might return to useful positions in the community. To oversimplify: society wants men to be taught to use liberty wisely while deprived of it.

What contribution can I now make to the pursuit of the rule of law? I have said I was the director of the federal prisons for twenty-seven years, from 1937 to 1964, and I believe these memoirs of my experiences will be relevant. In fact, the federal prison director is the man closest to the crime crisis. He is, to put it baldly, the whip hand of the courts and the keeper of the keys. He is the punisher, the deterrer, and the rehabilitator. His job is to devise and manage a system of corrections that really corrects. His purpose is to help society—and to help control crime—by turning as many lawbreakers as possible into productive citizens.

The federal prison director must oversee a federal prison population of about twenty-five thousand men and women in thirty-six institutions that range from massive penitentiaries to prisons without bars. He must provide leadership for a career service of five thousand prison employees, administer an annual budget of more than sixty million dollars, and coordinate more than two dozen prison industries with an annual profit of five million dollars. He must endeavor to set pilot examples to state and local prison systems. He must be available as a sort of journeyman expert on all forms of crime. He must serve as an authoritative witness before congressional, lawyers', and civic committees on such issues as capital punishment, trial by jury, juvenile delinquency, sentencing procedures, narcotics, treatment of women offenders, firearms controls, medieval cruelty in state prisons, civil disobedience, and the menace of uncontrolled protest.

The federal prison director is no source of power in his own right. I was specifically answerable to U.S. attorneys general as totally different from one another as Homer S. Cummings, Frank Murphy, Robert H. Jackson, Francis Biddle, Tom C. Clark, J. Howard McGrath, James P. McGranery, Herbert Brownell, William P. Rogers, Robert F. Kennedy, and Nicholas deB. Katzenbach. I was appointed and reappointed by Presidents Franklin D. Roosevelt, Harry S. Truman, Dwight D. Eisenhower, John F. Kennedy, and Lyndon B. Johnson.

The prison director is, in fact, the public servant most likely to become a whipping boy. He has only to suggest that the men and women in his charge have hearts, minds, and lungs, and he is accused of "coddling convicts" or "running a country club at the taxpayers' expense." He has only to intimate that some criminals harbor evil designs, and he will have to listen to the strictures of sociologists who say that prisons are brutalizing agents and only the ignorant or the sadistic would ever get into that kind of work.

These memoirs will therefore state a position on the crime crisis that is factual, objective, and founded on what I trust to be unalloyed professionalism. I believe I know and understand people in prison—at least from the view of custodian, confidant, and mediator—better than most men. I believe I also know society's interest: that men emerge from prison filled with hope, not hate, and that they are received in similar spirit. Such men will be less likely to commit new crimes, to inflict new losses upon society.

There can be no question, the current uproar about the crime rate notwithstanding, that notable progress in the treatment of offenders has taken place.

In 1937, the year in which I became federal prison director, more than two thirds of the men released from federal institutions were sent back to some prison for fresh offenses.

In 1964, the year in which I retired, only one third of federal prisoners were returned for new commitments.

This halving of the recidivism rate in the federal system is one form of batting average by which any conscientious prison director might measure the fight against crime. And because the 1930's (the Great Depression) and the 1960's (crime in the streets) have been lawless eras of roughly comparable violence, the difference may best be explained by the growing success of our prison reforms and our emphasis on rehabilitation. The halving of the federal recidivism rate is even more remarkable when it is considered that seventy per cent of the men sent to federal prisons have previous convictions. In other words, the U.S. Prison Service has *proven* able to take a cross-section of "hardened criminals" and "tough young punks" and turn two out of three into citizens who are not sent back to prison.

This has been a victory won by teamwork, continuity of purpose, and a reasonable view on the part of all the law enforcement agencies, in contrast to the suspicion, jealousy, and outright conflict that are now beginning to pervade the atmosphere.

Our prison reforms started in the 1930's from the premise that applies dramatically to the 1960's: What makes a criminal is in large part lack of education. Whatever it is that causes men to quit their schooling—and miss out on most of the opportunities of life—is what sets up the magnetism of crime.

No fewer than 54.7 per cent of our felony inmates in the

federal system did not go to high school, and another 27.6 per cent were high school dropouts. By contrast, 12.4 per cent of felony inmates were high school graduates, 4.2 per cent had one to three years of college, and only 1.1 per cent were college graduates. An important motivation toward crime is lack of education, using that term in its broadest sense—religious education, moral training, character building—not lack of intelligence. The IQ levels of the felony inmates were comparable to the national averages.

The federal prison records also show that unskilled men outnumber the skilled men overwhelmingly. More than two thirds of felony inmates were laborers, service operatives, and unskilled hands of various types. One in six were blue-collar craftsmen and foremen. One in six were white-collar clerks, salesmen, professional men, and technicians. These percentages have held good, incidentally, in the five years since my retirement.

The single most important contribution American families can therefore make to the fight against crime is, factually speaking, to stimulate their boys' interest in their education and development of skills of every type. Boys? Another fact about the crime crisis is that women offenders, for all the garish publicity that surrounds them, are few and far between. Only one woman is arrested in the United States for every eight men and only one woman goes to prison for every twenty-five men.

Similarly, the most important contribution the prisons can make to the fight against crime is not to punish but to educate. The prisons ought to provide education in useful skills and in orderly ways compulsorily, with stern discipline and no possibility of escape. This re-education will qualify the prisoners for a law-abiding life much more logically than solitary confinement, the whip, the striped suit, the bread and water diet, and all other accoutrements of "tough prisons."

The educative approach toward the convicted offender *works*. I have said we were able to cut the recidivism rate in the federal prison system in half. I have also ascertained in interviews with men who have succeeded on the outside, and with others who have been returned to us, that a broad and constructive program of prison education and work skills is one of the two decisive factors of rehabilitation. The second factor is the extent to which men's families and friends help them reestablish themselves after their release. Specifically:

Prisoners who have taken advantage of industrial, academic, and other vocational training programs are twice as likely to succeed after release as those who have not.

Prisoners who have, in addition to retraining, worked for regular hours and regular pay in the federal prison industries, are five times as likely to succeed as the others.

My professional experience indicates, therefore, that it is wholly possible to bring about the inner changes in the minds of convicted men so necessary to their self-esteem, self-discipline, and self-reliance. I believe it is society's interest that we try. Too many of our prisoners tell their wardens at the start of their prison experience: "Oh, what's the use. Nobody thinks I'm any good." It is even difficult to convince them they have anything within themselves worth saving.

Imagine the great prison doors clanging shut. The men approach their ordeal, stirred, bewildered, and fearful. They are stripped, fingerprinted, photographed, bathed, and disinfected, and they are in torment. It is in this moment of their deepest trouble that they find their need for honest guidance and friendly counsel.

Even today a prison sentence is tough medicine. It takes men from their families and friends for extremely long periods. It imposes a lifelong stigma. It confines them to a few dreary acres and enforces a monotonous clockwork of hours. It clothes them in cheap uniforms from which individuality has been expunged. It destroys their privacy and clusters them with fellows they might loathe. It deprives them of normal sexual relationships and imposes a temptation toward homosexuality. A prison sentence at its worst amounts to a refined torture much harsher than corporal punishment.

The argument in favor of tough prisons is that they deter others from committing major crimes, although this has yet to be proven and may never be. Even more primitive punishments of the past are still with us, with little effect. When we are told we are coddling convicts and we ought to crack down, are we being urged to return to corporal punishment, to the lash of Judge Jeffreys of the Dorchester Assize, who used to order floggings with gallows humor? " 'Tis a cold morning for madam to strip," he said. "Be sure to warm her shoulders thoroughly." The lash is still in use officially in two southern states and informally in several others, and there is no more evidence of its effectiveness now than then.

Are we to return to the traditional prisons of the early nineteenth century, as defined by Warden Rose of the state of Maine: "They should be terrifying, dark and comfortless abodes of guilt and wretchedness. No mode of punishment is so well adapted to prevent crime and reforming a criminal as close confinement in a solitary cell, cut off from all hope of relief, furnished with a hammock on which to sleep and a block of wood on which to sit. There his vices and crimes will be personified and appear to his frightened imagination as covenants to overwhelm him with horror and remorse." More than a hundred of our prisons were built before the Civil War, and New Jersey's state prison at Trenton, in particular, in use since 1798, is a national disgrace.

After many years in charge of the federal prisons, I can hardly be accused of being naïve. I am well aware that some of our prisoners are violent, vicious, unregenerate enemies of their fellow men. But many more are physically and mentally handicapped, the unwanted and unneeded, the disadvantaged and the dropouts who perceive no merit in completing their education. When the population of the local jails is analyzed, my point is incontestable: more than seventy-five per cent of the men and women in the lockups are drunks, vagrants, mental defectives, drug addicts, and other social misfits who ought to be in clinics, not jails.

The true course to follow in our pursuit of the rule of law, is rehabilitation, not retribution, and the cry for blood must not prevail. Prisons will serve our purpose in prosaic ways, by providing for medical care, religious instruction, routinely scheduled work, vocational training, academic education, sure discipline, psychological guidance, family visits and correspondence, the provision of an organized life on a timetable. Prison staffs will manage an "individualized system of discipline, care and treatment," as required by the founding statute of the federal Bureau of Prisons in 1930. And, as I shall show in this book, there are many more things we can do.

President Johnson challenged us in his last months in office to seek more fundamental solutions. He said, "There are very few affluent and educated Americans who are attracted to crime, and very few that have criminal records. But as we bring a fairer measure of prosperity and education to our 32 million poor people, I believe that the crime rate whose growth frightens us will begin to shrink significantly."

Similarly, President Richard M. Nixon, in the spirit of his Quaker forebears, says that no national fight against lawbreakers can succeed if we neglect to treat the headwaters of the causes of crime.

On the walls of my office in Washington are three paintings that symbolize men's efforts to accept or reject the rule of law as they see it. Opposite my desk is a picture in a modern mood, bought from a life-termer in our former maximum-security prison on Alcatraz Island in San Francisco Bay. It is called *The Dancing Swans* and, given a little imagination, two spritely birds may be seen flying freely away into the sunshine. On another wall is a copy of Norman Rockwell's wonderful painting of a doleful sheriff, with scraggly hair and bulbous nose, listening to a boy behind bars playing the harmonica. The boy is trying to play his way out of jail.

The third picture haunted me during my long years in the

prison service and still looms up before my thoughts as I write. It is a copy of a surpassingly grim Van Gogh—the penitentiary yard, the drab tones of despair, the confinement of spirit, the prisoners paraded in that futile, endless circle, the dark shadows cast by pitiless walls, the preposterous officials in their hats looking on.

What not to do to men.

THE MAD,
CLANGING BELLS
OF PRISON

*Even the mentally normal find it barely tolerable to
be shut up for a day, or even an hour, with people
who grossly annoy or disturb them.*
                    The Lancet, British Medical Journal

One night after I returned home from an inspection tour around
the federal prisons, I was awakened by the telephone ringing
beside my wife's bed. A moment of relief. I was in my own
room in Bethesda, Maryland. I was not a prisoner—the subject
of recurrent nightmares for me—in one of my own institutions.
My wife picked up the telephone and I listened in a half-sleep
to her end of the conversation. "Yes," she said, "but Mr. Bennett
is sleeping. I don't want to wake him up.

"Why should I shine a light in his face?

"I see . . . but the prison officers have to do that to make sure there's a man and not a dummy in the bed.

"I'm sorry you want to get even . . . I'm sorry you feel that way."

I was wide awake by now, and I asked my wife who was calling just as she put down the receiver. She said it was a former prisoner who wanted me to know how it felt to have my sleep interrupted twice a night by somebody shining a light in my face. The guards at the federal penitentiary at Lewisburg, Pennsylvania, had done that to him for fifteen years. My wife said: "The man said he didn't blame you personally, but he thought you ought to do something about it. He said you don't realize how unnatural prison life is."

As I tried to get back to sleep, I thought to myself that the man was probably right. I have talked with thousands of men who have spent from a few months to fifty years in prison, and I slept in as many cellblocks as possible to get an inkling of what life in one of our penitentiaries was like. Although I closed down as many of these bastilles as possible and opened several prisons without bars, the traditional walled institution is still the core of our correctional system. Anyone who seeks to rehabilitate criminals and help them back to useful lives must venture behind bars to find the men who want to make the attempt. But I could never fully comprehend the prison experience, because my presence there was voluntary and experimental. I was free to leave any moment I cared to. I knew I could never really measure the men's resentment at the petty details of the regimentation to which they were subjected.

Take the matter of bells. The men ask with appalling frequency why it is necessary to ring so many bells in prison. They say it almost drives them out of their minds. A bell jarring them awake at 6:30 A.M., and another a half hour later telling them to stand at the doors of the cells to be counted. A bell for breakfast call, and another bell for return to quarters to make beds, mop up the floors, and listen to special instructions. Then a bell for the work crews to assemble, and so on through the long day.

A prisoner once broke off an interview with me and shouted: "Bells for this! Bells for that! More bells than Poe could dream up! Bells for noise! Bells for silence! Bells for every goddamn thing!" He launched into a stream of obscenities.

Bells all day and lights in faces at night are necessary, as even the most ardent prison reformers know, because there is no other safe way to maintain order and keep the operations of a penitentiary running smoothly. Prison discipline requires that each man be in the right place at the right time, and this is also sound rehabilitation. Hideouts and escapes must be prevented. Shirkers and malingerers must be watched. The movements of violent inmates, sex deviates, and confidence tricksters must be accounted for. This is quite a job when two or three prison officers are often responsible for the supervision of several hundred men in the big cellblocks and groups of dormitories.

Small wonder that the population count is an elaborate event at most prisons, which may be repeated at intervals throughout the day. When the bell is sounded, the men in each area—cells, workshops, schools, athletic fields, etc.—are lined up and counted. Doors are closed so that no prisoner can slip out, or cover for another man. Each officer, when his count is completed, phones the result to a control center where all the returns are consolidated. When the prisoners are reported "all present and accounted for," another bell is rung, and activities are resumed.

The prison officer about to inaugurate some new form of rehabilitation program—never more determined in his life than now to help his fellow men—might suddenly find himself confronted with a prison population that is bent on "screwing up the count." One man will hide out, screw up the count, and listen with savage glee to bells jangling all over the institution. Then he will reappear in his appointed place, in time for the recount, with an excuse for his absence that cannot be disbelieved.

In the prison underlife—in which prison officers and prisoners must meet and interact if there is to be rehabilitation—the mores are those of any totalitarian society. Values are distorted, perspectives are warped, and distinctions emerge out of the imposed conformity. The community is isolated and ingrown. Trivialities that would pass unnoticed in the outside world are endowed with extravagant significance. Small worries become colossal fears. Gossip and rumor are currency. Somehow the prisoners take the greatest pleasure—and the guards seem to pick up the tempo—in finding out what they believe to be the intimate details of the lives of the wardens, judges, parole board members, not to mention their own attorneys. They become morbidly fascinated with one another.

The prison officer's first dilemma—assuming he is a conscientious man—is how far he may reasonably go toward identifying himself with his charges, if only to understand them. It will probably occur to him that, "There, but for the grace of God, go I." But if the officer indulges this emotion, if he allows a prisoner to become aware of the compassion he feels, will he destroy his usefulness as an individual responsible for all the other prisoners? The prison officer, according to the manual of regulations, ought to remain impassive and fair, and he should not question his role as society's agent in guarding the men who have transgressed.

When the underlife imposes its conditions, the prison officers lose their freedom to maneuver. Prisoners are hypersensitive and insecure, and they are especially touchy about their prerogatives. They may not be deprived of these without trouble, even for their own benefit. Early in my career I wanted to change a rather simple procedure at Alcatraz that struck me as being unfair to most of the men. The cooks and washers who worked in the kitchens were allowed to prepare and eat their own meals, and this meant they received far more than their share of the rations—"eating on the range," it was called. But when I attempted to enforce our regulations providing for a standard poundage of food per man per day, also meaning per cook per day, I ran into serious trouble. The whole prison population stood behind the cooks and washers to protest the removal of privileges, and I decided not to make an issue of it at that time. Later we reduced the number of men eating "on the range," then eliminated the custom altogether.

In the federal penitentiary at Leavenworth, Kansas, the situation was more serious. We removed a group of Italian-American prisoners from their work assignments in the bake shop, in which they were idling away their sentences. There was an uproar. It turned out that the bakers had been preparing excellent breakfast rolls for all the prisoners and unless we agreed to send them back to the shop, we would have to face the threat of a hunger strike. When the ringleaders demanded that the bakers must also be allowed to work with only minimum supervision and draw unlimited amounts from the pantry, the time had come when we had to assert our authority. So we quietly picked up one after another of the troublemakers and bundled them off to Alcatraz. We also decided that the bakers needed training in other skills. But the tension lasted for weeks.

The prison officers, casual visitors, judges, newspaper reporters, and the prisoners wonder whether we ought to differentiate our treatment of prisoners. Should we make life miserable for kidnappers, narcotics peddlers, and enemy espionage agents while we allow the bootleggers, gamblers, or income-tax violators to have an easy time of it? But the consensus is that men should be allowed to serve their time with as little reference as possible to what has gone before.

Morris "Red" Rudensky, who served a long term in the federal penitentiary at Atlanta and made the grade back to a vice president of an advertising agency, recalls his own attitude:

"You glance at dozens of other new prisoners as you are marched through the large prison yard to the initiation ceremonies in your new well-guarded abode. You wonder how the prisoners you've noticed can behave so naturally, just like people outside behave. They didn't look like the grim-visaged cons on the screen of your favorite neighborhood movie house.

"This place must be full of guys like yourself, you tell yourself, and maybe it's not so bad after all. You're absolutely right. The place is chock-full of guys like yourself, no better, no worse.

"You answer a few routine questions and you're recorded in the prison files. It happens in every prison, you're told. You're fingerprinted, mugged, measured, weighed, numbered, given a shower, anointed heavily with lice-killing blue ointment and then issued your first prison suit. They clipped your hair in former years but this sanitary and depressing hairdo is now passé in better prison circles. All the new guys are all together, of course.

"The dress-in ordeal over, you're led to your cell by another prisoner. It has finally happened to you. You're in, brother! You look your new home over very carefully. There's really not much to see. It's small, cold and strong. Not much more in your cell than there is in a zoo cage.

"Unconsciously, almost, you begin to pace back and forth. You feel trapped. Countless millions of prisoners have felt as you feel now. Trapped. You walk two or three steps forward, the same number back. Since that day, I've walked thousands of miles in cells during thirty-five years in prison. Good exercise, but bad for your nerves, if you're treading on time.

"Everything takes time and you have plenty of it (remember?) to clear your mental decks and fit your attitude and emotions to this strange new environment. Slowly, it begins to dawn on you that days pass into weeks, weeks into months, and months into years. The pendulum drags slowly. So you begin to tinker with it."

In the penitentiaries, there are the realists, the men who are able to accept their sentences with the knowledge that time passes, freedom is inevitable, and the interim must be handled with a minimum of unpleasantness. There are men who construct shells of indifference and, for years, nothing moves them.

There are tough guys bent upon vengeance, easy to identify with their boasts, "This is their day—I'll have mine." There are guilt-ridden prisoners, obsessed with repentance, and others who slip in and out of sanity. Many more lethargic men serve out their time as mindless automata, reacting only to the signals of prison routine.

Prison officers instantly recognize the man who is constantly cheerful and optimistic for no good reason. As another of my prisoners, Stanley E. Mockford, described this type: "His grin appears to take on a gruesome stiffness after a time, and his humor a brittle falseness, but he persists in wearing his ludicrous mask and uttering his blithe inanities until one wonders if his skull houses the mind of a dolt."

Mockford writes on: "The prisoner who has evolved a personal method of overcoming the more obvious difficulties of prison life, utilizes many devices to occupy his mind. Light reading is the commonest resource, or writing, about anything. Or conversation. Painting becomes an obsession for some men and so absorbed do they become in their hobby that time sometimes races too madly. Bridge seems to intrigue many. Building castles in the air. Daydreams. Sports—including the endless compiling of sports statistics and facts. Sleep is the great narcotic. In slumber, a prisoner is free—a circumstance that leads some prisoners to develop a great capacity for oblivion. They drift away into unconsciousness shortly after they reach their cells and live on a schedule divided between work and sleep."

But every man who goes to a penitentiary must serve his sentence one day at a time. He must define his relationships in the underlife even if he does not choose to play a direct part. Similarly, prison officers must also try to penetrate the closed society, and they must know the makeup and motivations of the cliques, how they operate, who are the leaders, and how they exert pressures.

One of the first challenges for new prisoners, assuming they do not go it alone, is to try to make a place for themselves with the other men. Sometimes the "snow job" is crucial to this process: how to impress everybody with one's potential importance. The new men learn the basic prison vocabulary and use phrases like "bum beef" and "bum rap" as they spread their line of talk about previous experiences. They build their images, perhaps, by hinting they have been "drydocked" several times, and they talk knowledgeably about how hard the wind blows at Lewisburg, about the quality of the food at San Quentin Penitentiary in California.

If they are interested in these newcomers, the influential prisoners might offer gestures of friendship accompanied by casual demonstrations of power. They might be able to procure better-fitting shirts, for example, by bribing guards or trustees in the clothing office; the price would be "a pack or two." Even though they know they can get fresh clothing merely by asking for it, the new men often choose to go through the ritual.

Then the influential prisoners might ask the new men if they want to write to women not on the approved correspondence list and, in prison parlance, if they want to "kite" letters out of the penitentiary without inspection. A guard might do this, but it would take "real money." But perhaps a certain trustee in the business office might be persuaded to slip illicit letters into the official mailbag, also for "real money." In the federal prison system, there is a five-year penalty for anyone caught passing contraband out of jail, but seldom is anyone apprehended. There are too many places to watch and too few people to do it.

What is happening is this: the new prisoners are seeking to belong to the society that exists; the society is seeking the allegiance of new men to its rules, thereby to perpetuate itself. Men with long sentences almost always want to belong, while the prison-wise with short terms tend to stay aloof. They insist, as they phrase it, in "doing their own time." Youthful prisoners, however, are apt to join, because "You need friends to talk to in here," and "Friends help you do time easily." Perhaps one in three new prisoners tries to make a few friends.

What is also happening is that prisoners are achieving this closing of ranks almost without reference to authority. They are adapting to the new life and devising their own self-protection rather than accept the help of the prison officers. They strengthen and refine this security by forming cliques and even "families" within the mass of the prison population, and sometimes they develop loyalties that amount to fanaticism. The unforgivable sin in the American penitentiary is still to "rat" or "snitch" on a comrade.

The prison society has an elaborate range of punishments for violation of the convict codes. A disagreeable man loses a cherished belonging, and a braggart is left out of card or checker games. A sluggard who does not keep his share of the cell clean is dumped in the mud, and a man who does not bathe is held under a shower until he is half-drowned. A prisoner who snitches on a minor matter reports to the infirmary one day with a broken nose that he incurred, he says, in a "fall."

A prisoner who rats on a big deal becomes ill with symptoms of panic. He is frightened out of his wits and he has to be sent to another prison for his own protection. The weapons of the underlife are fists and clubs, home-made knives, whips made out of anything long and hard, rocks, buckles, and shapeless objects that fall from heights on people's heads. Over the years, we have managed to stop the practice of "kangaroo courts," however, in which the prison society even put its own offenders on trial.

In this situation, prison officers find they must enforce stern discipline if they are to begin meaningful rehabilitation efforts. They may observe some minor infraction "through the bulkhead," but they must never let the men mete out their own rough punishments. Prison officers therefore set up their own organization from their own espionage networks, and do their best to head off trouble before it starts. The officers in the federal system are strictly forbidden to use anything resembling direct action or anything that could be construed as corporal punishment, however. They do not, partly because this is undesirable and also because it is less effective than removal of privileges, a job change, or canceling treasured visits.

The prison director's ultimate sanction against recalcitrant prisoners is the removal of "good-conduct" credits, which renders them ineligible for parole and lengthens their stay in the penitentiary for months and perhaps for years. Even the prisoners with hopelessly long sentences fear this punishment not only because it restricts their privileges but also because they never lose hope that a way out can be found.

The wardens in charge of each prison in the federal system are responsible for the maintenance of discipline. Their associate wardens are usually in charge of dealing out minor punishments. Three-man disciplinary boards, comprising the associate warden and the senior staff officers of the custodial and the medical-psychiatric divisions, are convened to handle more serious offenses—fighting, homosexuality, assaults on prison officers, and so on. While I was prison director, Washington had to approve any withdrawal of good-conduct credits.

In practice, the wardens find they obtain better discipline by offering incentives: A warden's good word or favorable testimony before a parole board is the utmost a prison officer can do for men facing long sentences. The associate wardens have the dominant voice in work assignments, including the allocation of jobs in the federal prison industries, in which men are able to save their pay to help provide for their dependents, or to use when they are released.

Thus the prison officers control their institutions absolutely. There is none of the balance of power depicted by some novelists. To be sure the prison society has its way of enforcing its rules. Gambling, for example, is illegal in federal prisons, and properly so, since it is second only to homosexuality as the source of fights, stabbings, and unrest. Welching on a bet, however, is a sin to be avenged by some subtle method, such as planting dope or a knife beneath the offender's bed and tipping off an officer. Yet gambling persists in baseball and football pools, poker, gin, dominoes, and the numbers racket. The currency is "the pack" or "the carton." The men are allowed to spend fifteen to twenty dollars per month in the commissary and they buy cigarettes and use them as spending money. But whenever the prison officers try to crack down on gambling, they seldom find tell-tale evidence and they learn little. The gamblers give up their sugar-cube dice or policy slips for a time and meanwhile place their bets on such insignificant events as the numbers of the hymns the chaplains will call out at Sunday morning services.

The University of Illinois–Ford Foundation research project of the early 1960's, headed by Dr. Daniel Glaser, conducted a sort of popularity contest in the federal prisons, among much else. The researchers asked the prisoners which category of officials they liked most and least, and why. The psychological caseworkers were disliked, possibly because they were regarded as snoopers, and so were the officers directly responsible for administering discipline. The popular officers were usually the cellblock guards, with whom the men came into the closest contact, and the work supervisory and vocational training instructors, who were trying to teach skills. The researchers found many prison officers were able to communicate extensively with prisoners, and that the personality of particular officers was often responsible for many men's rehabilitation. As one man said about his work supervisor:

"He was a nice old man and, when I left prison, he shook hands with me and said, 'You big son-of-a-bitch, if you come back to this place, I'll kill you, much as I like you. You don't belong in this place.' There were tears in his eyes as he said this."

Similarly, model prisoners can be decisive influences in the penitentiary. One of these was an Army colonel who served a life sentence at Atlanta and Lewisburg for murdering a man he had thought to be involved with his wife. I first became acquainted with the colonel when the yard captain pointed him out at Atlanta one day and said: "Looks like the colonel's getting into bad company." The colonel was talking with a bank robber and notorious troublemaker in the penitentiary, "Rewrite Eddie," so named because he had once been a newspaperman. The two men were speaking earnestly and at length.

Not long afterward, an anonymous letter brought us word

that many of the men in Atlanta were about to launch a work stoppage. The warden thought that Rewrite Eddie was the ringleader. The morning of the day designated for the strike passed without incident. Then came lunch hour. Two thousand men filed into the dining hall and took their places at the tables. But when the food was served, they sat with folded arms and would not eat. Somebody was about to start a demonstration. The deputy warden rang the bell to order everybody back to their cells, but no one moved. The men were all looking at Rewrite Eddie, who had maneuvered himself into a front row seat on the aisle. He was the man who was going to give the signal.

Suddenly, the colonel rose from his seat at the back of the dining hall and walked up the aisle and looked down at Rewrite Eddie. There was complete silence as the colonel caught the younger man's eye and gave him a cold, hard stare. Then the colonel turned and, as if he were on parade, walked down the aisle and back to his cell, alone. It was an act of great courage. The warden now knew what was happening: the colonel must have known about Rewrite Eddie's planned strike for weeks and had been trying to talk him out of it. Minutes ticked by until Rewrite Eddie got up and trailed away down the aisle, followed by a few others, then by the whole prison body. The colonel had prevented a damaging strike and, as it turned out, he had also saved Rewrite Eddie. The young man lost his leadership in the prison society and concentrated on rehabilitating himself for his eventual release.

Shortly afterward, the colonel was transferred at his own request to Lewisburg so he could be closer to his family. Soon the warden there noticed that the colonel was seeking out troublemakers and urging them to make something of their lives. The colonel advised one aggressive youngster from New York City to stop baiting prison officers and take up baseball, at which he was quite proficient. "The colonel kept talking baseball with me, and I got started playing on his account, I guess," the boy said. The colonel suggested to a former organist, a petty criminal and an alcoholic, that he ought to study music again. The man said, "I'll do my time and get back on the street where I belong." But the colonel kept pounding at him until he volunteered to play once or twice at Catholic services. Soon he was playing at all the services and he gave Bach recitals during recreation periods.

The colonel's most unexpected success came when he persuaded a man with a twenty-five-year sentence, a hopeless case who had been contemplating suicide, to try some part-time work as a teacher in the prison. Within six months, the man found a role for the long years teaching illiterate prisoners how to read.

Soon the colonel's influence at Lewisburg was almost akin to the warden's. One day while visiting the penitentiary, I was chatting with the warden and the colonel. The warden said to the colonel, "It's Christmas, and it's pretty tough to have to spend Christmas in prison, under any circumstances. Do what you can to make it as pleasant as possible for the men. Colonel, I'm beginning to think you've accomplished more around here than any of the rest of us. It's getting to be an old story. A guy's in trouble. He straightens out. Then your name comes up." The colonel replied, "My life isn't worth much to me personally any more. Maybe I can help someone else."

He was paroled in due course, but died within two years of his release. "Prison has changed me greatly," he wrote me. "I have had ample time to transfer my surviving ideals from precarious pedestals to less elaborate and more substantial bases. I retain, and prize, my self-respect."

This is what prison reform is all about.

THERE BUT FOR
THE GRACE OF GOD

BE IT ENACTED *by the Senate and House of Representatives in the United States of America in Congress assembled.... That there is hereby established in the Department of Justice a Bureau of Prisons ... responsible for the safe keeping, care, protection, instruction and discipline of all persons charged with or convicted of offenses against the United States.... The said institution is to be planned and limited in size so as to facilitate the development of an integrated, federal penal and correctional system which will assure the proper classification and segregation of federal prisoners according to their character, the nature of their crime, their mental condition and such other factors as should be taken into consideration....*

... in providing AN INDIVIDUALIZED SYSTEM OF DISCIPLINE, CARE AND TREATMENT ...

> *Act approved by President Herbert Hoover, Washington, D.C., 1930*

When I submitted my first draft of this famous statute to Sanford Bates, who was soon to become director of the new bureau, I was feeling uneasy and self-conscious. I was a junior employee in the Justice Department. Bates was formerly commissioner of corrections in Massachusetts, and the foremost prison reformer in the country. Bates looked at the draft carefully, and asked: "What do you mean by individualized treatment? Will the Congress and the public really want to treat prisoners as separate personalities with their own problems? And what do you mean by an integrated system? Will the wardens and their officers be led toward a single goal?" Bates put similar questions to me as he tested my knowledge of the material before taking it to Attorney General William D. Mitchell.

A few days later, Mitchell called Bates and me into his office and said he had discussed the prison situation with President Herbert Hoover. The President said the purpose of prisons was to restore, redeem, and reach the hearts of men—and in this light, society's needs could be more clearly seen. Hoover, a Quaker and a humanitarian, approved the new federal prison bureau and secured its adoption by Congress. Bates was the first director, and I was to be the second seven years later. Hoover, in that act, laid the rock upon which we were to found a generation of prison reform. Thirty-five years afterward, President Johnson echoed Hoover's tones when he said: "The best law enforcement has little value if prison sentences are only temporary and embittering waystations for men whose release means a return to crime."

Today the United States has the largest prison population of any nation in the world—at federal, state, and local levels. More than 400,000 people are actually locked up in prison on an average day—220,000 felons, 140,000 misdemeanants, and 40,000 juvenile offenders. About 25,000 men and women are held in our federal institutions, more than 200,000 in the state prisons, and the rest in local jails and workhouses.

There are some 400 penal institutions in the country, 21 holding more than 2,000 inmates apiece. Four state prisons are the largest, with an average population of 4,000 or more. These are California's San Quentin Penitentiary, the Illinois state prison complex at Joliet and Stateville, the Michigan State Prison at Jackson, and the Ohio State Penitentiary at Columbus. There are also 220 state-operated institutions for juveniles and 83 locally controlled youth houses and reformatories. There is very little policy coordination between the states and the 3,047 counties and towns that run their own lockups. These range in size from New York City, Los Angeles, and Chicago—jails with four to five thousand persons—to small New England jails, with one or two inmates. The federal government has no jurisdiction outside its own prison system, even though it encourages everyone to adopt its goal of "individualized discipline, care and treatment." Inspectors of the federal Bureau of Prisons do, however, visit local jails and prisons where federal prisoners are boarded to see that approved standards are maintained.

The proliferation of prisons, jails, and police lockups and the lack of uniform purpose mean that it is difficult to set national standards. Moreover, ideas differ widely across the country as to how discipline should be maintained, work accomplished, and fights, riots, and homosexuality suppressed. In 1967 I testified in federal court hearings in Arkansas, called to determine whether whipping in the state prison farms was "cruel and unusual punishment." The superintendent and other officials of the Cummins and Tucker farms admitted in court that men were whipped with leather straps about four inches wide, nailed to a wooden handle, and were lashed on the bare buttocks until the skin was broken or the officer's heart softened.

This practice went on unchecked until a federal court ruled that no more than ten lashes were to be laid on at any one time, and that "civilian" officials had to be present at whippings. But the prison guards circumvented this ruling by administering the lashes in more than one dose, according to court testimony. They also ordered trustie prisoners to beat the victims with shovels, hoe handles, chains, blackjacks, and tractor fan belts. If the men resisted, they were spread-eagled by four trusties and "stomped," suffering loss of teeth, broken bones, and fractured skulls.

One of the prisoners was a seventeen-year-old boy who had been sentenced to eight years for stealing an automobile. He had not been able to plant seed tomatoes as fast as the trustie fore-man demanded and had been whipped. He told me he did not know how to plant the tomatoes and the trustie would not show him until he shared the eight- or ten-dollar monthly allowance he received from his tenant-farmer parents. This allowance had not been enough to buy a shirt he needed and to pay an older prisoner to keep the "wolves" out of his bed at night. He had taken his whippings until finally he asked for the intervention of the federal courts.

Another of the prisoners, in on a bad-check charge, told the court he had been whipped because he had not gleaned his okra vines properly. "Overlooking okra" was the unforgettable phrase. He testified he had a sty on his eye and could not see the leftover okra. An ophthalmologist was even brought to court to rule on the boy's excuse, and he said it was possible that the boy was telling the truth. The trustie simply said that a touch of the whip was a good cure for eye trouble.

Then there was "Tuckers Telephone"—a dread instrument of torture in free use at the Tucker farm for "reformable" young men. This was a generator from an old crank telephone, a couple of dry cells, and some wires. The boys who were punished by being "called up" on Tuckers telephone were strapped to a table, with sets of wires tied to their feet and their sex organs, and the current was passed through their bodies until they fainted.

How many prisoners were murdered or shot while allegedly trying to escape will never be known. I remember the story of Rufe Persifal, a federal prisoner in the 1930's who was known as "The Buzzard" because he could rifle down buzzards on the wing. Persifal had been a trustie at the Arkansas farms and had shot three men "trying to escape." Each time he was granted a special pardon by the governor, but he could not stay out of trouble and he finally committed a federal crime. We sent him to Alcatraz, where we could protect him from the vengeance of other prisoners, and where there was a chance he would not be found some day with a knife in his back. But the end of the story was that Persifal, for some dark personal reason, cut off his trigger finger.

As a result of the federal court hearings and a state police investigation, an Arkansas state penitentiary study commission recommended improvements in a wishy-washy report. The commission apologized for the whippings by noting that a whip, or lash, was not used—only a heavy, leather strap nailed to a handle. Finally they agreed that "the use of the strap is not necessary" and recommended that it be abolished. Meanwhile Governor Winthrop Rockefeller forbade whipping and other abuses without even waiting for the commission report.

Then some of the prisoners told the authorities there had been many murders on the prison farms and that men were buried on the grounds. When bodies were found exactly where the prisoners said they would be, a new round of investigations got under way. But the Arkansas state senate greeted this news by cheering a former convict who spoke and answered questions for three hours in the senate chamber. There was nothing wrong with whipping and electric shock treatments, the man said, and the prison farms were among the finest in the nation.

This example of medieval justice has since been found by the federal court of appeals to be cruel and unusual punishment and therefore outlawed by the U.S. Constitution. Chief Judge Blackmun of the Eighth Circuit in speaking for a unanimous court wrote: "The strap's use . . . offends contemporary concepts of decency and human dignity and precepts of civilization which we profess to possess. . . . Humane considerations and constitutional requirements are not, in this day, to be measured or limited by dollar considerations or by the thickness of the prisoner's clothing."

The grisly revelations of the Arkansas prison system hardly came as a surprise to me, nor to anyone even vaguely acquainted with the history of penology in the southern states. Beatings, lashings, bludgeonings, and murders of prisoners in the midst of unspeakable living conditions are commonplaces of penal history in the Delta region of the Mississippi River. The convict lease system, which did not disappear from the South until the 1920's, provided cheap labor for the mines, plantations, and lumber camps as well as revenue for the states. And when the convict lease system was abolished, state prison farms were established in Mississippi, Louisiana, Texas, Arkansas, Alabama, Georgia, and Florida in a vain effort to make prisons profitable. Each of these produced its own tales of exploitation, brutalization, and degradation.

While these conditions were condoned by most southern legislatures, the governors and budget directors of many northern states also let poor facilities and programs cramp the rehabilitation of offenders. But there has been some progress in some state prisons in recent years. The institutions of Wisconsin, Connecticut, California, and Michigan are clean and humane and make earnest efforts to improve the lot and the prospects of the inmates. Few states have improved as fast as Florida and Missouri. Florida has done away with its chain gangs and sweat boxes and is grappling with its overcrowding problem. Its able prison director, Louis L. Wainwright, has won the support of governors and legislators for the rehabilitation concept. At the time I studied Missouri's prisons in the late 1950's, knifings, riots, and petty graft were widespread, and eight or ten men were usually jammed into cells suitable for two or three. But the St. Louis *Post-Dispatch* prodded citizens' groups, the courts, and the state legislature into action, and funds were made available for new prisons, personnel, and parole facilities. Governor Warren Hearnes brought in my former deputy, Fred T. Wilkinson, as the new state director of corrections, and major changes were made. Under Wilkinson's leadership, the dilapidated cellblocks of Civil War vintage were torn down, food services were modernized, and work and training programs expanded. Wilkinson handled his disciplinary problems intelligently and humanely and is meriting national attention and regard.

It must also be emphasized that there has been progress in the disciplinary practices of all the states since President Hoover inaugurated the federal Bureau of Prisons. Before that time, corporal punishment was legally permitted in Alabama, Arkansas, California, Colorado, Delaware, Indiana, Kentucky, Louisiana, Mississippi, Missouri, Tennessee, Texas, and Virginia. Colorado even used the ball and chain! The federal prison wardens were allowed to handcuff men in solitary confinement to the bars.

Today, the federal system really has abolished all forms of physical punishment and does provide individualized treatment. We have an amazing range of institutions grouped around the traditional penitentiaries. There are maximum-security prisons, wall-less correctional institutions, farm and work camps, all types of medical and psychiatric clinics, even pre-release centers, in which selected men work and sleep outside the prison community in advance of their parole.

The big federal penitentiaries at Leavenworth and Atlanta are used for the confinement of men with long records of criminality. Their populations are approximately twenty-two hundred to twenty-five hundred. In the western states, there is a smaller and aged close-custody penitentiary at McNeil Island, Washington, accommodating another thirteen hundred long-term prisoners. The new penitentiaries at Terre Haute, Indiana, and Lewisburg, Pennsylvania, are designed for the treatment of the more hopeful men with long sentences, and they hold from thirteen hundred to fifteen hundred each. There is also a new maximum-security prison at Marion, Illinois, designed to harbor the more violent and escape-prone young offenders who are being sent to prison in increasing numbers for bank robbery, kidnapping, and assault. A year before I retired I replaced the most famous of all American prisons, Alcatraz Island, in San Francisco Bay. I closed Alcatraz in 1963, as I shall explain in a later chapter, because it was too costly to operate and too typical of the retributive justice that has no place in our philosophy.

The federal correctional institutions are at Danbury, Connecticut, Milan, Michigan, Sandstone, Minnesota, Tallahassee, Florida, Texarkana and La Tuna, Texas, and Terminal Island, California. These are intended to hold short-term offenders as close as possible to their homes, so that their families and the vocational training resources of their communities can be utilized in rehabilitation. There are numerous youth institutions, reformatories, and work camps and the Robert F. Kennedy Youth Center at Morgantown, West Virginia, as well as the prison without bars at Seagoville, Texas. About four hundred women prisoners are held in the women's reformatory at Alderson, West Virginia, and about two hundred women at Terminal Island, California. The federal system also tries to set an example to the states by segregating as many narcotics addicts and mentally ill prisoners as possible, accommodating them in separate institutions.

One of the misconceptions about prisons is that they are filled with sadistic murderers, desperate gunmen, romantic cracksmen, and cunning swindlers. In fact, the "big shots" amount to no more than one in ten of our population. The rest are what I call "eight-ball Willies," and the typical prisoner has never made more than fifty dollars out of a single crime. He is a young auto thief riding off in search of his El Dorado, or a fool who would risk ten years in prison to get ten dollars out of a drug store cash register. Donald Clemmer, a noted criminologist as well as chief of the District of Columbia prison system, once remarked that any successful citizen could commit a crime more efficiently than ninety-eight per cent of the "eight-ball Willies" behind bars.

The federal prison intake of about thirteen to fourteen thousand men each year falls into a score of categories of offenders and hundreds of personality types. There are approximately three thousand auto thieves, two thousand bootleggers, fifteen hundred forgers and twelve hundred narcotics offenders, along with a miscellaneous lot of counterfeiters, bunco artists, draft evaders, customs violators, postal thieves, embezzlers, stowaways, and a handful of perjurers and pornographers. Most of the really tough bank robbers, about four hundred to five hundred a year, are sent to federal prisons. We get about fifty kidnapers, forty rapists, and fifty men convicted of various forms of homicide. Fewer than two hundred income tax violators are sent to federal prisons in an average year for falsifying returns or failing to pay.

It is much more difficult to catalogue our prison intake by personality traits. A considerable number are unfortunates who never had a decent chance in life, and they are good-natured, tractable, and easy to guide. A small group are bitter, hostile, and depraved, and their danger to the other prisoners is extreme. There are misshapen, retarded, emotionally disturbed men whose problems are unsolvable. Finally, we have the cynical, the self-seekers, the rebels, the perverted, some of whom may be changed while others seem impossible to redirect considering our present lack of expertise and after-care facilities.

The length of sentences served by federal prisoners is roughly comparable to the national averages—averages, because the difference in individual sentence patterns in the state and local courts is considerable. In the New England states, for example, sixty-five per cent of defendants are placed on probation, while only fifteen per cent are given this second chance in Iowa. About fifty per cent of all federal offenders are granted probation. Our states have not yet managed to develop common criteria for measuring the harmfulness of different crimes, and the federal courts, as I shall show in a subsequent chapter, are far more consistent in their sentencing policies.

Until recently, in the Middle District of Pennsylvania, federal courts were handing down an average sentence of forty-four months for auto theft, as compared to an average of twelve months in federal courts in Rhode Island. But this is nothing compared to the disparities between the states. A rapist in Connecticut serves an average of twenty-one months' imprisonment, while across the state line in New York the average term is fifty months. Killers in Texas, even with malice aforethought, serve an average of two years nine months' imprisonment. In Ohio, they serve an average fifteen years two months.

How well, then, does the federal sentencing system work? Most of us are familiar with the scene, if not from personal experience, in which the judge asks the defendant if he has anything to say before sentence is pronounced. Usually, the defendant says nothing, or very little. Then the judge looks at his records, ponders what the defendant or his lawyer has said, and then pronounces a sentence. It can be a fine or imprisonment, or he can suspend sentence and place the defendant on probation.

The judge does not arrive at that decision on the basis of hunch, or, at least, I hope he does not. He has before him, on his bench or in his chambers, a pre-sentence report on the defendant supplied by probation officers. This is now required procedure in all federal criminal cases and is customary in most state and larger city courts. This pre-sentence report contains all the salient facts about the offense and a case history of the man on trial. This will include the man's personal and professional history, as far as it can be determined in the time available, and all previous convictions that can be traced. Sometimes, this pre-sentence report will include the comments of qualified people who might know the defendant, or who might possess some insight into his offense. Usually, the report contains a recommendation from the probation officer with regard to the sentence, but not always. Occasionally, the probation officer will urge imprisonment and specify the term to be served.

With this information, the judge passes sentence. If the defendant has no previous criminal record, and if his crime was neither violent nor "heinous," nor one where deterrence of others is a primary consideration, he is apt to be given probation. More and more courts are using the probationary technique and increasingly skilled personnel are proving the value of "the second chance" in controlling crime. Probation, I should make clear, is not so much releasing the offender as prescribing an alternative method of treatment in which the offender himself will decide whether or not he will change his ways.

The defendant who is not placed on probation is sentenced under one of several procedures. In some state courts, the definite-sentence system prevails. In federal courts and in many state courts, the judge has the discretion of setting an indeterminate term. The defendant with a definite term to serve usually becomes eligible for parole after completing one third of this sentence.

The federal courts and a number of state courts are increasingly using the method of the indeterminate sentence. The judge sets a maximum and minimum term, or merely a maximum term, and leaves to the parole board, or adult authority, or youth authority, the responsibility of setting the exact date of release. The theory of the indeterminate sentence is bound up with prison reform. The judge is not able to predict how well the man will do in prison, how soon his attitudes will change, and how soon he may be released in his own and in society's interest. So the judge postpones, in effect, the determination of the exact length of the sentence, and delegates it to the experts who observe the man's own progress.

In the federal courts, until recently, eighty per cent of all offenders plead guilty, and it is safe to say that across the country more than eight out of ten defendants plead guilty as charged. In many of these cases, a deal has been agreed to behind the scenes. The prosecutors want to obtain speedy convictions and the defendants, all too often, wish to avoid exposure for more serious offenses and make a deal with the prosecutor. None of this protects the public. Nor is it good justice.

If the defendant is sent to a federal prison, he is escorted by a U.S. marshal to that institution in which he stands the best chance of obtaining treatment suited to his individual needs. The Bureau of Prisons in Washington makes this decision. During his first month, he lives apart from the other prisoners while he passes through a vital phase known as "classification." He receives physical examinations and is interviewed, repeatedly, by custodial officers and social caseworkers, the chaplain, the psychologist, and a battery of specialists from the academic and vocational training divisions. They prepare a study for the use of a classification committee, composed of the senior officers, which sets the shape of the new prisoner's life. They decide where he will work and where he will be housed, whether he is to be kept under supervision as an escape risk or weighed as a potential honor prisoner. The committee then outlines a voluntary, individual schedule of education and recreation suited to the man's needs. They encourage him to take this course, and do well at it, and they remind him that progress will be an essential element to be considered when the time comes for parole.

The classification committee observes the man's progress and welfare and defines new goals as the months pass by. Then, in conjunction with parole officials, they begin to make plans for his release. Marital, parental, employment, educational, legal, and financial information is compiled for presentation to the parole board. The man appears before the parole board and states his own case for his release, whereupon the board decides whether to let him out of prison or to retain him for further treatment.

The performance of the community "after-care people" and the "family unit" immediately after the man's release from prison is, along with retraining in prison, the principal weapon society has in its fight against recidivism.

This godlike role for prison officials and various categories of experts outside the prisons imposes a high responsibility upon men and women who are all too human and susceptible to making highly visible mistakes. One misjudgment—and prison reform loses ground in a community. One man released from prison too soon might mean a woman raped or a bank held up at gunpoint. One man released from prison too late might mean a hopeful individual turned manic-depressive, useless to society, and a perpetrator of much more serious, violent crime.

There are more than 120,000 correctional workers in the United States today to discharge these awesome responsibilities. Of this considerable force, some 63,000 are supervisors and custodial officers, meaning that about a half of our prison personnel are kept busy guarding the prisoners, watching the walls, patrolling the cellblocks, and supervising work, meals, and recreational activities. There are 33,000 technicians and maintenance men and women who keep the plants running smoothly, and 17,000 case managers who follow the men from classification to parole and keep in touch with their families. Finally, there are 7,000 specialists—vocational and academic instructors, psychologists and staffs, doctors and nurses—who contribute their specialized skills.

This prison staff is hardly sufficient to take care of prisoners in most regions of the United States. The average officer-to-prisoner ratio in the country is one to seven, ranging from one to three in New England to one to two hundred in Arkansas, where trustie prisoners are used for most custodial duties. State adult institutions usually offer starting salaries for custodial officers that average twenty per cent less than salaries paid to local police. Caseworkers might get two thousand dollars or so more. Senior prison administrators receive perhaps twice as much as the caseworkers. Perhaps six out of ten institutions try to find superintendents who are college graduates. More prison workers are needed, of course—perhaps eighty thousand more by 1980—and specialists are particularly required.

It is wonderful news that eighty-eight per cent of the prisons in our country claim they offer academic educational programs, for example, but there is only an average of one accredited teacher for every 225 men. We try to handle this problem by inviting well-educated prisoners to conduct classes, and teachers and college-educated housewives who live near the prisons are asked to volunteer for part-time instructional work.

The federal prison system is attempting to set an example in personnel as well as program management. The federal prison service is a career organization that I helped establish. Each recruit must have civil service classification. Usually, he is a high school graduate, with some college, and he is paid as much as a police officer. Salaries rise to the scale paid to wardens of the large federal prisons, who earned approximately twenty-five thousand dollars a year in 1967. One new proposal indicates the new importance of prison work. There is under consideration a National Academy of Corrections, in which the prison specialists of the future will be trained, West Point style, for their role in the fight against crime.

In the biggest prison system in the world, however, progress is often achieved in disorderly and unpredictable ways. It is possible that one young robber did more to improve the Massachusetts prisons, for example, than anyone since Sanford Bates. He was a federal prisoner named Teddy Green, who served time in sixteen jails, detention centers, reformatories, and penitentiaries before he was finally committed to Alcatraz.

Teddy Green's father was an immigrant from Greece who lost his savings during the Depression. Teddy was brought up on the south side of Boston, where the racketeers were the idols of the unemployed. At the age of thirteen, he went to see the old Edward G. Robinson movie *Little Caesar*, in which Robinson dies like a hero under a hail of machine-gun bullets. Teddy brought with him an imitation scroll-sawed and painted submachine gun and, at the end of the show, he let out a wild whoop and ratatatted the gun at the audience. There were screams and a near-panic, and Teddy was arrested and sent to reform school as a juvenile delinquent.

Teddy was a smart, engaging lad who soon won release, only to be returned to his own neighborhood, where he was shamed and shunned by the parents of his old friends. To impress and win back some of his companions, he stole a car, and he was caught and sent to a reformatory. The next time, it was armed robbery and a sentence of imprisonment in the grim old state institution at Charlestown, a nightmare of a place that reformers had been trying to close down for decades. Teddy escaped, bundled up in a bale of rags, and he robbed a bank soon after his getaway. This brought him under federal as well as state jurisdiction.

After his recapture, Teddy was returned to Charlestown, where he was held while his attorney appealed his state case. After this, he was to be sent on to the federal system. During these months Teddy was locked up in the maximum-security Cherry Hill block with condemned murderers. They were kept in solitary confinement in semi-darkness, sleeping on stone floors, subsisting on bread and water shoved twice a day through six-inch slots in the doors, and they were allowed out only once a week for showers.

One day in 1955, Teddy and three other long-term prisoners seized five of the Cherry Hill guards as hostages. They demanded to be released and threatened to kill the guards if they were not let go. There were signs of hysteria in Boston. "The prisoners are defiant—they have nothing to risk," one radio commentator said. "A prison chaplain says they are not afraid to die. They are armed with pistols and shotguns. The yard of the ancient bastille is alive with bazookas, gas grenades, heavy-duty revolvers and two machine guns. The ringleader, Teddy Green, has threatened to kill the five guards if one gas bomb is thrown or one shot fired."

But no gas bombs were thrown, no shots were fired, and, after eighty-five hours, the governor and the warden agreed to appoint a committee to hear the prisoners' grievances. Teddy and his men let the hostages go, and the siege of Charlestown was over. Out of the reports and recommendations that followed the hearings came the changes that reformers had long sought. Brutality was stopped, living conditions were improved, and early in 1956 the hulk of the prison was abandoned forever.

Thus passed one of our worst "embittering waystations of crime"—but was Teddy Green to be considered a hero? Perhaps not. After he arrived at Alcatraz, however, Teddy changed, and he became his own redeemer. So great was his improvement over the years that the Massachusetts authorities agreed to take him back to serve his state sentence concurrently with ours. There he won the respect of the parole board and, on my solid recommendation, he was paroled and set free. Now Teddy Green is a successful salesman in Boston.

IV

"CAN THIS BE A CIVILIZED COUNTRY?"

One evening in California not long ago, a federal judge, a prison warden, and I were sitting around the dying embers of a barbeque fire on the ranch of that most prolific and successful writer of detective stories, Erle Stanley Gardner. It seemed strange to Erle, as it has to others, that anyone who is free to stay away from prison would choose to spend his life guarding and helping those who had broken the law. Erle's voice took on a booming, biblical quality as he asked me: "Tell us in all candor, Jim, whether there is any satisfaction or reward in being your brother's keeper."

Before I could answer, Federal Judge George Boldt said he assumed I had gone into prison work more or less by chance. "But why did you continue in this career once you knew about the kind of people you'd have to deal with?" Warden Preston

Smith said with a smile that I must have been fascinated by the glamour of public office.

My mind went back to Washington in 1919. I went there for the first time not long after deciding that flying a Curtiss Jenny in the United States Army Air Corps had no real future for me. I admitted I would never get the hang of where the controls of the Curtiss changed while I was doing a barrel roll or a tight eight. I had better give up flying, I thought, before I got a fuselage with silver handles on the side, the kind of coffin we aviation cadets grimly joked about. So, when orders came to our squadron in Montgomery, Alabama, to discharge anybody who wanted out, I put in my request. Not long afterward, I was passing through Washington on my way home to Rhode Island. There was the majestic dome of the Capitol—and I was thrilled in some indescribable way. I knew then and there I wanted to come back to Washington and work for the government. I had no idea how I might accomplish this, and it did not occur to me to analyze why I was interested in public service.

My father was an Episcopal minister, and that might have had something to do with it. There were prayers every day and almost all day Sundays, and I was encouraged to set myself standards of conduct. My family was poor, and I was concerned about the problems of my fellow men. I was taught to make up my own mind on important questions and to learn from decisions that turned out well or badly. I was never "indoctrinated" in public service, however, and my explanation to Erle Stanley Gardner and the others that evening in California was that I more or less grew into the discipline.

I was born in Silver Creek, Chautauqua County, New York, in 1894 and my memories have a turn-of-the-century quality that is sometimes difficult to explain. Horatio Alger really did sum up the mood of the new generation. Parents were dedicated and youngsters were deserving and families for the most part pulled together. My mother and father, on an income that never exceeded eighteen hundred dollars per year, managed to put me and my two brothers and three sisters through a high school eight miles from home, and all of us after that through four years at Brown University.

Even though society had its ways of helping clergymen, we had to help ourselves. Mother boiled clothes, stewed salt pork, and cleaned oil lamps. She also arranged church plays, dinners, and socials so that my father could "resurrect" the church treasury. All the children had to work passage. On a cold evening, Mother would point to the needlepoint that hung behind the Rochester stove in our sitting room, embroidered with the words "The Lord Will Provide." She would quip, "The Lord provides for those who provide for themselves. Please go and get some coal and put in a shovel full of cinders."

The memories of those days are dear to me. Sometimes I look at my father's photograph in our family album, taken with my mother at Niagara Falls about the turn of the century. Mother always used to tell me what a wonderful place "the Falls" was whenever she tried to persuade me to save some more pennies in a highly decorated teapot she had bought on that trip to Niagara. She kept a second teapot from Niagara Falls on a high shelf. There she treasured the special fees that my father earned by conducting weddings and other functions, earmarked for the trip she hoped to take one day to her ancestral homeland, the Netherlands. Sometimes she took down the teapot and showed me the dozen or so $2.50 gold pieces or bills, the $5.00 pieces and bills, and, once, an envelope containing a single dollar bill. "See, Jamie," she said. "Your father is right when he says 'Look out if the fee comes in an envelope. Its always small.'" She had to wait until her seventieth year before she went to the Netherlands.

Ours was an educated home, and we were omnivorous readers and learners. My father could repeat long passages of Shakespeare verbatim. My mother, once a schoolteacher, enjoyed giving him advice and ideas for his sermons. Once, she took a line out of Shakespeare and suggested he use it for his text. The line was: "He jests at scars who never felt a wound." Many years later, when I was about to begin my career in the federal prison service, she brought out the penned manuscript for the sermon and said it might inspire me in my new work.

As a boy, I plunged into stories of heroes struggling against odds. I reveled in the Henty books, *The Last of the Mohicans*, and *Wild Animals I Have Known*. I found myself drawn to stories about great humanitarians rather than great warriors, although I hoped that good men of peace and war were joined in noble purposefulness.

I saw my first crime when I was ten years old, not long after my father moved to the parish of Sodus, New York, a small town near Rochester. One morning my father took me to see a safe that some burglars had blown open in a local store. The cracker-barrel fraternity of the town was on hand. The proprietor was trying to add up his losses and answer the questions of the local newspaper reporter. Our constable, who doubled as a cobbler, was poking around the room telling everyone he was expecting a detective from Rochester any moment, who would solve the crime. I stared in bewilderment at the heavy safe door, blown off the hinges by dynamite, and at a mass of horse blankets used to deaden the sound of the explosion. The scene was mysterious and exciting to me until Father explained that the victim of the crime had been ruined and would have to close his store. Then it all seemed so unfair.

Oddly enough, I ran into the Sodus safe-cracker thirty years later when a man in the Lewisburg Penitentiary complained he was getting inadequate medical attention and asked if I could do anything to help. I noted from the prison records that he had admitted the Sodus robbery as his first job, and had spent most of his life in prison on an assortment of burglary charges. A chill passed through me as I realized I could not be objective in this matter, and I would do nothing to help him. I sent along the complaint for others to handle and did not inquire what, if anything, was done.

Not long after the Sodus robbery, my father accepted a call to be assistant rector at St. Paul's Church in Burlington, Vermont, and my first childhood resentments toward those who harm innocent people were forgotten. In Vermont there were wonderful, fun-filled times. The winters were freezing, and a steamlike fog rose over Lake Champlain as it iced over. Skating and ice-boating on the lake were thrilling adventures for us. In those days, there were few ski trails near Burlington or anywhere else in the state. Occasionally, we would get some flexible white pine slats, tie them on our feet with leather straps, and pole ourselves down the hillsides. Nobody was very good at this, and we preferred to ride a barrel stave to which a twelve-inch high seat was nailed. We scooted down the slopes much faster than those few boys who had "sissy skis."

The really good days were in summer, and our favorite game was "kick the wicket." Seven or eight twelve-year-olds would go out every evening after supper and play "kick the wicket" on a street corner at the end of the block. The game was fairly simple. A broom stick would be slanted up against the curb. Somebody would kick the wicket as far as he could and run to base on the next corner. If he could get there before another boy retrieved the wicket and replaced it against the curb he was safe. Often there were arguments and we would ask the paunchy Irish policeman on the beat to decide whether a boy had really touched base, had kicked the wicket contrary to the rules, and so on. All of us accepted his rulings without question. The policeman was one of us.

One evening, our friend did not appear on his beat and we could not figure out what was wrong. Then Father told me that the policeman had been shot by a man he had caught climbing out the window of a neighbor's house. He was dead. For weeks, the boys talked it over, and we could not understand why anyone would kill such a man. The policeman carried a billy, and twirled it magnificently at the end of a rawhide thong, but never a pistol. It was unfair, and all we could do was to run up a collection of pennies for his widow and store our fury. The murderer was never found.

We left Vermont for a country parish in Greenville, Rhode Island, in the fall of 1906. I entered an ungraded school not far from my father's stone church several miles from town. These were the days when the horse and buggy was gradually giving place to the automobile, but we still traveled by stage coach to the end of the trolley line, or we walked four miles there and back.

There were wonderful characters in Greenville. There were men who never let alcohol touch their lips and those who patronized "the bungalow," the speakeasy for the community, which always voted dry. There were women who never lifted their skirts above their ankles and there was a town prostitute who could be had for a quarter. There were generous souls like "Uncle Charlie," who once gave me fifty cents for two hours' work throwing wood into his shed and tightwads like "Farmer Seth," who gave me a quarter for three days of pitching hay. My mother once dictated to me a letter to Farmer Seth, sending back a quarter, saying that he needed the money more than me.

I remember how it broke my heart when the town librarian, a lady I secretly admired, had a sordid affair with the cashier of our local bank. Everyone was shocked when the bank closed its doors and the couple was nowhere to be found—"gone to Timbuctoo" was the expression. A great deal of money had been taken, but then as now in cases of white-collar crime the problem was handled discreetly. Nobody went to jail. The townsfolk criticized the directors, who had been careless and would have to make up the deficit. The auditors were "the fools." I hoped nothing unpleasant would happen to the librarian, but I was very troubled by such casual tolerance. If a poor man had committed a like offense at his level of society, he would have been hounded down.

In the autumn of 1914 I entered Brown University and began to work my way through college. On weekends I was a butcher boy in the public market in Providence, making fifteen cents an hour, and I saved everything I was given or could earn. In school, I was not able to master trigonometry in my first year, got a D in Juvenal only because I was able to memorize most of "the trot," and really surprised myself by getting a B in German. I received a warning from the dean, but this was less of a crisis than it would be today. There were no men on the waiting list, and our great and eloquent president, W. H. P. Faunce, had to travel about the country recruiting students in person.

That was how my future wife, Marie, happened to enter Pembroke, the women's college associated with Brown. She was persuaded by the dean of women to come to Pembroke after she had completed high school in Hackensack, New Jersey. The dean of women also paid a call on Marie's father, John Ettl, a sculptor who had emigrated to this country from Hungary, and told him about the advantages Pembroke would have to offer— presumably including the opportunity to meet Brown men.

Brown suddenly began to pick up for me. Academically, the tide turned. I met Marie at a Kappa Sigma initiation party and we had fine times together. I also joined in the preparedness programs of pre-World War I, drilling enthusiastically with my comrades on the back campus with wooden guns. The Lafayette Escadrille—Norman Prince, Bert Hall, Kiffin Rockwell, Victor Chapman, and the others—inspired us all. After I graduated from Brown, I joined the Army Air Corps, but not in time to see action. I was still a "cadet aviator" with the rank of private second class and the salary of thirty dollars per month at the end of the war.

In short order, I got my honorable discharge from the Air Corps, married my Pembroke girl, and went back to Washington to learn whether I had the necessary qualifications for a government career. I took the civil service examinations and passed. Then I was assigned to the U.S. Bureau of Efficiency, a forerunner of the subsequent Hoover Commissions designed to help streamline the federal bureaucracy. I also attended law school at George Washington University and received my degree.

My first real opportunity came in my fourth year in the civil service when Herbert Brown, chief of the bureau, asked me if I would like to be assigned to the Department of Justice to study the federal prison system. The purpose of the study would be to show that penurious Vermonter, John Garibaldi Sargent, attorney general in the Coolidge administration, that the country could save money by putting idle federal prisoners to work. I knew this was an important and controversial topic. A cardinal tenet of prison reform is that fruitful work engenders self-respect and encourages a prisoner to redeem himself. The argument against prison work is that products of low-cost labor, thrown on the market, can undercut the products of free men. I was in favor of prison work programs but I was aware that organized labor was hostile and that my study would have to be expert and invulnerable. Probably, my report would be sent all the way to the White House.

Before accepting the job, I read every book about prison industries I could find, especially by such authorities as Harry Elmer Barnes, Dean Kirchwey of Columbia University, Samuel Gompers, Warden Lewis Lawes, and others. To gain additional seasoning and insight, I set out on a tour of some typical state prisons, starting at the Ohio State Penitentiary at Columbus. There occurred what was probably the decisive experience of my early career.

My first view of the antiquated institution was frightening and foreboding. When I looked at the stone prison, with its high walls and its bristling towers patrolled by riflemen, I lost some of my desire to present my letter of introduction to the warden. Through the bars that surrounded the reception area I could see several groups of gray-clad men marching about silently. The prisoners had large numbers inked on the backs of their rough, wrinkled shirts. It was a depressing introduction.

After what seemed like an unnecessary delay, I was ushered

into the office of Warden Thomas. He sat at a bulky, square oak desk that had large, round, carved legs. The desk seemed as solid as the stones of the prison wall. Thomas checked my credentials, asked to be remembered to a congressman we both knew, and sent for a guide, who, I thought, was to take me around the workshops. Later I learned he was a former treasurer of the state who had put his hand in the till. "Show Mr. Bennett around and bring him right back here." I thanked Thomas and followed my guide into an interior courtyard perhaps fifty yards across, where I saw a line of men moving across the square in a long, skating stride, each man with one arm on the shoulder of the man in front of him. This was the famous "lockstep." The prisoners moved rapidly without a sound other than the shuffle of their shoes on the walk, and their eyes were focused on the ground.

My escort was pleasant, but he volunteered no comment on prisoner attitudes and prison disciplines. He showed me around the tailors' shop, the weave shop, and the machine shop. They were poorly lit, filled with obsolete and worn-out equipment. Many of the prison workers were squatting against the walls of the rooms or loitering by the drinking fountains. The prison officers in charge of the workshops were positioned in chairs on platforms elevated three feet above the floor, heavy clubs in their hands. Every now and then, a guard would pound his club on the platform and point at a prisoner, or shout an order, and the prisoner would seem to understand. I thought the prisoners looked dispirited and hopeless, but the guards could not be blamed.

The enormous cellblocks depressed me beyond measure. One of them housed, as I recall, more than nine hundred men, with two prisoners in every ten-by-five-foot stone-walled cubicle. My guide commented that he lived on the top floor of this block, and that it got damned hot in summer. As we walked down one corridor, I saw several men in their cells pacing up and down with unusual intensity, jabbering to themselves, rattling their bars, or shouting obscenities. The officer told me to pay no attention to these men; they were "psychos." They were kept in the cellblock with all the other prisoners because there was no other place for them. I wondered whether this was really a civilized country in the second decade of the twentieth century, but there was more to come.

Warden Thomas welcomed me back to his office and began to talk. He said that his was an extremely tough job, and he was not too impressed by "softies" and "do-gooders." And although he was in favor of prison industrial work, he did not see how much of a goal could be made of it because there was not enough of a market for prison products in the state agencies. The unions—"the laborskates"—had too much power. As for the prisoners, they were getting what they deserved. At this point, I asked Thomas how prison officials maintained discipline and how they punished offenders. "Come with me," Thomas said. "I'll show you."

We strolled back across the square to a small brick building. Thomas banged his fist on a wooden door, and it swung open. We walked into a small, dark room with a high bench at the far end. This was his "court room," Thomas said, where he and his deputies sat in judgment upon prisoners who violated the rules. The punishments were loss of visiting and correspondence privileges, loss of good-behavior credits, and "the hole." Thomas added that "the hole" was right in the building. "Open up, officer, I'll show Mr. Bennett." A barred, steel door was unlocked, and, after that, a steel boilerplate door. Through both doorways we went into a narrow corridor lined with more steel doors, and Thomas motioned to a guard to open one. There stood a pathetic creature, his eyes staring vacantly, his hands handcuffed to a bar halfway up the wall.

"What are you here for?" the warden asked the prisoner. "I put in a 'cop-out' to see you, sir," the man replied. "How long have you been in here?" "Five days." "I don't believe you," Warden Thomas said, and he hurried me on down the corridor.

Next, he showed me the cells reserved for prisoners who refused to work or were otherwise recalcitrant. These men were
stood for hours or for days in tiny strap-iron cages, in which
there was no room for them to sit down, until they agreed that
washing pots and pans or shoveling coal was not such a bad
fate. I did not argue with the warden or ask any more questions.
I had seen enough, and I never wanted to get out of a place so
badly in my life. Half-heartedly, I thanked Thomas for taking
the trouble to show me around and headed for the gate.

After this experience, I canceled the rest of my inspection
schedule, and was therefore spared the sight of what Minnesota
State Prison and the Leavenworth Penitentiary must have been
like in the mid-1920's. I went home to spend the weekend won-
dering whether I could accept this kind of assignment and
whether I could be of any assistance. We were dealing with
atrocities.

My wife had few doubts, however, that I ought to persevere.
She had done some social work in Harlem years before, and she
seemed excited by the concept of prison reform. Here was
something that perhaps our generation might accomplish. She
did not see why prisoners were treated like wild beasts and why,
so degraded, they should be turned loose upon society only to
commit new crimes. She was concerned about the plight of
prisoners' wives and families, who were penniless, shamed, and
shunned. Nor did Marie understand why prison labor could not
be utilized constructively, perhaps to make products for sale to
state agencies, so as not to compete with private markets.
Finally, Marie asked a question in almost the same words Erle
Stanley Gardner used beside his barbecue so many years later.
She said, "Why *not* be your brother's keeper?"

On the following Monday morning I reported to Herbert
Brown at the Bureau of Efficiency and told him about my visit
to Ohio State Penitentiary. After I had finished, Brown asked
if I wanted to continue with the prison study assignment. He
was a considerate man, and he had a formula ready for me. I

could turn down the prison job without detriment to my future. Another assignment would soon be coming up, he said, to investigate the supply procurement systems of the Veterans Administration, and I could go to the VA if I'd rather.

"Thanks," I said, "but I'll stay with the one you gave me."

So I chose prison.

1,700 LASHES

My decision to enter the prison service thus came about more
or less by happenstance. Once I had made the decision, however, I knew I would pursue the cause of prison reform as if it
was a call. Within two years, I was able to recommend, write,
and help get passed the laws that led to the first federal Bureau
of Prisons. I would later take charge of all the federal prisons
and change most aspects of prison life. As I saw it, my obligation was plain:

> *I was in prison, and ye came unto me.*
> *And the King shall answer and say unto them, Verily I say*
> *unto you, Inasmuch as ye have done it unto one of the least of*
> *these my brethren, ye have done it to me.*
>
> Matthew xxv. 36,40

I recognized that there had been progress in the administration of justice in the Western World during the three hundred years since a shipwrecked sailor, crawling on to the shores of England, spying the gallows and gibbets on a nearby hill, exclaimed: "Thank the Lord for bringing me safely to a Christian and civilized land." In the United States of the mid-1920's, boiling in oil, disemboweling, the severance of limbs, the death of a thousand cuts—all forms of judicial torture—were not practiced. Instead, the American passion to punish expressed itself in terms of imprisonment of savage length. Then, within the prisons, men were routinely strung up by the thumbs, handcuffed to high bars, kept for weeks in solitary confinement on bread and water, were whipped, paddled, and spanked, spread-eagled in the hot sun, locked up in sweatboxes, confined in tiny spaces where they could neither lie nor sit nor stand. It could be argued that Western man had progressed from the days of the feudal system and it could be argued he had not progressed very far.

In this situation, it seemed to me that what progress had been achieved was the work of men of action. Humanitarians, yes, but skillful and talented men and women who had attained a point of power from which they could exert leverage. If I was to accomplish anything, I would have to be able to insist on change. And the times were in my favor. In the mid-1920's, a civil service career was neither lucrative nor prestigious, and so few young men were entering the prison service in particular that the field was wide open. It was perfectly possible for a neophyte lawyer and bureaucrat to recommend major changes that would be carefully considered by his superiors and might well be put into effect. When President Hoover replaced Calvin Coolidge in the White House, there was a new emphasis upon humanitarian legislation—and the great Quaker watched over the careers of young humanitarians in Washington with personal interest.

It was therefore not naïve for me, nor a waste of time, to look

back across the centuries, to study the lives of the prison reformers of the past, to frame my own recommendations in the
light of the torch they had placed in my hands. It took little
intelligence to realize that I was involved in a continuity of
thought and action. Charles Dickens, for example, after his visit
to the "model" Eastern Penitentiary in Philadelphia in the mid-
nineteenth century, reacted much as I had after my experience
at Ohio State Penitentiary. Dickens wrote:

"I am persuaded that those who devised this system do not
know what it is that they are doing, that there is a depth of
terrible endurance in it which none but the sufferers can fathom,
and which no man has the right to inflict on his fellow creatures.
I hold this slow and daily tampering with the mysteries of the
brain to be immeasurably worse than any torture of the body.

"I solemnly declare that with no rewards and honors could
I walk a happy man beneath the open sky, or lie me down upon
my bed at night, with the consciousness that one human creature, for any length of time, lay suffering this unknown punishment in his silent cell and I the cause, or I consenting to it, in
the least degree."

The message of the years was that the administration of
justice tended to be violent in the extreme, but the determination of the reformers was just as implacable. The lives of a
handful of men and women, unsurrounded by armies, had
changed history, and they inspired me as I began my work.

Cesare Beccaria (1738–94) was a temperamental Milanese
nobleman, one of several ardent young literary men "disgusted
with the wretched state of the economic organization of Lom-
bardy," who met in their homes night after night to frame
romantic proposals for modernizing their community. Beccaria
was allotted the special field of criminal jurisprudence, "perfectly adapted to a man of eloquence and lively imagination,"
and he wrote down his ideas on scraps of paper. The friends
strolled about in the Italian twilight and starlight discussing the
fact that torture was the basis of justice and that hundreds of

crimes were punished by revolting methods of death. They bemoaned the fact that the illustrious Blackstone, even, who had just published the first volume of his *Commentaries*, believed in witchcraft. "The thing," wrote Blackstone, "is in itself a truth to which every nation in the world hath in turn borne testimony."

Beccaria was neither a lawyer nor a criminologist, but rather an intellectual who brought to his subject the humaneness, courage, and enlightened curiosity of the Age of Reason itself. Man, as man, was of interest. Happiness was a desirable objective. The alleviation of the more grotesque of social abuses was fashionable. From Montesquieu, the young Italian developed the relationship of laws to the state of public opinion. From Hume and Helvetius, he derived a utilitarian view of ethics. From Voltaire, he learned about many of the specific cruelties in the several bodies of criminal law. With his friend and subsequent collaborator, Alessandro Verri, Beccaria visited the horrifying dungeons of Milan and, in July 1764, he published what is perhaps the most influential single essay in the history of justice. He called it *Essay on Crimes and Punishments* and his words are pertinent and timely today:

"The countries most noted for the severity of punishments are always those in which the most bloody and inhuman actions are committed—for the hand of the assassin and the hand of the legislator are directed by the same spirit of ferocity. . . .

"Crime is owing to the laws themselves. . . .

"The end of punishment . . . is no other than to prevent the criminal from doing further injury to society, and to prevent others from committing the like offense. In order therefore that every punishment may not be an act of violence committed against a single individual, it ought to be public, speedy, necessary, the least possible in the given circumstances, proportioned to the crime, dictated by the laws."

Beccaria's brilliance was surpassed by his reckless courage, for he went on to attack the Inquisition itself. He wrote of the inquisitors: "They are the ministers of the Gospel of Christ bathing their hands in blood in the name of the God of all mercy." The Inquisitorial Council of Ten met to decide what to do about Beccaria, and they decided not to arrest him, but to hire a literary critic to dispose of his point of view. The critic denounced Beccaria in the Milan journals as "a fanatic, an impostor, a madman," and the *Essay* was "unrestrained satire, perfidious chicane, dissimulation, specious fallacy and irrelevance." Beccaria himself had feared that his voice would prove too feeble against the noise of blind custom, even though the few wise men scattered about the earth might respond.

The spirit of the age was with Beccaria, however, and the *Essay* was a sensational success. Within six months of its translation into French, the *Essay* went through seven editions. Voltaire wrote a commentary upon it for the English language edition. Sonnenfels in Austria, Filangieri and Renazzi in Italy, Blackstone, Howard, Bentham, and Romilly in England were profoudly influenced. Reforms were set in motion in response to the *Essay*, particularly by Leopold of Tuscany and Maria Theresa of Austria. Beccaria was invited to St. Petersburg by Catherine the Great to help her draw up new laws, but he was ill and could not go. In the American colonies, Adams, Franklin, Jefferson, and probably Washington read the master work, and in the new country punishment began to tend toward imprisonment instead of torture.

The first great activist of prison reform was John Howard (1726–91), an English country gentleman with a bent for meteorology, who was serving as high sheriff of Bedford. After sitting through one session of assizes, Howard took the unusual course of inspecting the prisons to which he had just consigned some offenders. He was viewing these prisons from a personal perspective, having once been a prisoner-of-war in one of the campaigns against the French, watching 136 of his countrymen buried in a hole in a single day.

In Bedford, Howard moved carefully. He asked, first, why

several persons acquitted of all crimes were still held in jail. The answer was that they had borrowed money from the jailers while in prison awaiting trial and, despite their acquittals, they would have to stay in jail until they paid up. How could they make the money they owed? No one knew. So Howard suggested that the town authorities pay the jailers a salary and the acquitted men be released. This was acceptable to Howard's superiors provided he could furnish them with adequate precedents for such expenditure of public funds. So Howard went off on a tour of English prisons to find his precedent, and there he found evidence for a sustained attack upon his country's entire administration of justice. "Looking into the prisons," he wrote, "I beheld scenes of calamity which I grew daily more and more anxious to alleviate."

For seventeen years, Howard wrote books, pamphlets, and articles that aroused wide and influential interest. In Newgate, and elsewhere, there was little food, little water, and the atmosphere was so foul Howard had to air the pages of his notebook. There were virtually no sewers and no drains. There was no bedding unless the prisoners paid the jailers for straw. There was no work, nothing to do. There was no separation of prisoners by sex, age, or degree of criminality. According to Howard, the mentally ill prisoners "served as sport to idle visitants." New arrivals were greeted by the jailers: "Garnish (pay the jailers) or strip (to be whipped)." Howard wrote:

"If it were the aim of magistrates to effect the destruction, present and future, of young delinquents, they could not have devised a more effectual method than to confine them to our prisons, these seats and seminaries of idleness and every vice."

Within two years, Howard made quick gains. Several members of Parliament, sensing the public interest, pressed elementary laws. Prison walls were to be scraped and whitewashed at least once a year. All acquitted prisoners were set free. Prisoners who had no clothes were provided with them at public expense. Sick prisoners received medical attention. Underground dungeons were abolished and adequate ventilation assured.

Howard continued to inspect the prisons—his power was growing and he could not be kept from making sure the new laws were enforced. He stressed the need for new codes of reform and helped bring about the basic General Prison Act of 1791. Prisoners were given bread with beef on Sundays and a penny a day to buy "cheese, butter, potatoes, peas and turnips" from visiting tradesmen but never from the jailers.

Women prisoners were separated from men and juveniles from adults. Outdoor courtyards were paved and pumps installed. In each prison, an infirmary was provided with bedding for the sick and cribs for babies born inside. Workshops were set up, but felons were not put to work against their will.

Howard toured the prisons of Europe and was impressed by Pope Clement XI's house of correction in Rome, by the Maison de Force at Ghent and by several other institutions in Switzerland, Germany, and Holland. He translated Beccaria's dicta into specific terms when he reported that Holland, with a gentler system of justice, had a capital crime rate ten times less than that of England. He was heeded in the United States by the Quakers of Philadelphia, and also in Prussia, which in 1814 enacted a series of reforms based upon Howard's recommendations. But Howard's England by now was embarked upon the banishment of prisoners to Australia—the old version of solving crime by removing offenders from view. As William Eden wrote in his *Introductory Discourse on Banishment:*

"If there be any terrors in the prospect before the wretch who is banished to New South Wales, they are no more than he expects; the devoted convict naturally reflects that his crimes have drawn on this punishment and the offended justice does not mean to seat him for life on a bed of roses."

The Australian venture had begun in 1787, when Captain Arthur Phillip left England with a fleet of eleven ships bearing 1,051 persons, including 552 male convicts and 190 female convicts, a motley assortment of highwaymen, pickpockets, prostitutes, and penniless debtors. Phillip also brought the framework of a house for himself, tools and seeds, two pipes of port, 104 dozen bottles of wine, two puncheons of rum, twelve barrels of porter, 20 hundredweight of loaf sugar, 40 decanters, and 34 glasses. There was, however, no fresh clothing, no medicine, no reserves of ammunition for the marines in charge. There were no skilled tradesmen in the group, no farmers, no one who would know how to find food and shelter.

Small wonder that there followed twenty years of hunger, disease, and privation for the first Australians. It is understandable that the free settlers who followed the convicts were bothered by their lack of discipline and their thievery and that they demanded a crackdown. They complained that prison officers' whips were so soft the men laughed when they were flogged. The New South Wales governor agreed: "The cord may be sufficiently heavy, but it is of too soft a twist; although it bruises, bleeding is seldom caused, consequently the offender escapes that acute pain and smarting to the extent so desirable should be experienced under the lash."

The incorrigible prisoners who could not be controlled by the whip were sent on to Norfolk Island, a tropical paradise nine hundred miles northeast of Sydney Harbor. In 1834, a Catholic priest, Dr. Ullathorne, went to the penal settlement to console some men before their execution for their part in a rebellion. "It is a remarkable fact," he wrote, "that as I mentioned the names of the men who were to die, they one after the other, as their names were pronounced, dropped on their knees and thanked God that they were to be delivered from that horrible place while the others, those to be reprieved, stood mute and weeping. It was the most horrible scene I ever witnessed."

To this dreadful place in March 1840 was sent Alexander Maconochie (1787–1860), a retired naval captain, an improbable hero, a co-founder of the Royal Geographic Society, and private secretary to a colonial official in Australia. He had been asked by the Society for the Improvement of Penal Discipline, one of the offshoots of John Howard's reform movements, to obtain answers to a questionnaire about the penal system in Tasmania, then known as Van Diemens Land.

There he wrote: "The proper object of discipline is to prepare men for discharge. The first object of prison discipline should be to reform prisoners and then prepare them for advantage both to themselves and to society after discharge."

Appointed superintendent of the penal settlement on Norfolk Island, Maconochie issued a new set of regulations that were viewed as revolutionary. He dismantled the gallows on Norfolk Island and removed the protective bars from his own residence. He abolished the rules that ordered convicts to "cringe" before prison guards, and bade his charges to "stand up like men." He reduced the use of the lash, held open court on violations of prison discipline, refused to accept anonymous denunciations. Then he reorganized the prison body, weeding out the hopeless criminals, forming the others into working teams of woodcutters, carpenters, and farmers. He let the teams live in camps outside the prison settlement near their places of work.

Maconochie built two churches for the prisoners, in which he conducted services and read the lessons himself. He allowed the men to wear their own clothes, work their own plots, and sell their own produce at controlled prices, and he let them grow tobacco and smoke it. Not one year in office, Maconochie felt confident enough on Queen Victoria's birthday to hold a party unlike any Australasia had seen. The convicts were served rum and lemonade and they drank the Queen's health, after which they presented a theatrical performance.

Maconochie built schools in which his men were trained for employment after their release. And he developed his New System of Prison Discipline into five principles, each of them quite new. He proposed that a prison sentence should not be for a period of time, but for the duration of a task, of a determined and specified amount of work. This was the indeterminate sentence. Next, he defined a method of "marking" the prisoners in such categories as good conduct, frugality of living, habits of industry. The number of marks earned set the time of release.

While in prison, said Maconochie, a man should earn everything he received, except for shelter and subsistence. There should also be a trustie system, in which first-class prisoners formed "groups," and the whole group was held responsible for the conduct of each of its members. In the final phases of imprisonment, men ought to be subject to less rigorous confinement while emphasis was placed on their pre-release education —but they were still required to earn marks.

Maconochie succeeded beyond his dreams—a success that can be measured today in the sophisticated terms of the reduction of recidivism. During his four years at Norfolk Island, he set free 1,450 men, of whom only three per cent committed other offenses that brought them back to prison. Of his 920 supposedly irreconcilable "old lags," only twenty were reconvicted for subsequent crimes. Maconochie even attempted what we would now call occupational therapy.

One of the prisoners was a former naval rating named Charles Anderson, who had been transported to Australia for seven years for breaking into a shop. During his first fifteen months in Sydney Harbor, Anderson had been given a total of seventeen hundred lashes for various offenses and, for two years after that, he was tied to a rock in the harbor at the end of a chain twenty-one feet long. When his wounds became infested with maggots, he was untied and sent to work in lime pits. The pain of the lime on his lacerated back almost drove him insane. One day Anderson killed an overseer and he was sent on to Norfolk Island, sentenced to wear chains for the rest of his life. He was there, aged twenty-four, when Maconochie arrived.

Maconochie first sought to restore the man to his senses. He put Anderson in charge of some unruly bullocks and told all the other prisoners to leave him alone. Somehow, the bullocks

and the prisoner grew more tractable together. Then Maconochie stationed Anderson at an observation post on the highest
point of the island, where he served proudly as a lookout and
tended a small garden. Three years later, the visiting governor
of New South Wales saw Anderson, a telescope under his arm,
and asked, "What smart little fellow may that be?" Maconochie
replied: "That is the man who was chained to the rock in Sydney Harbor." But years afterward, Anderson went out of his
mind and died in an asylum in Sydney.

Maconochie was relieved as superintendent in 1844 and his
successors reinstalled the gallows and resumed floggings. This
led to a convict revolt in which four guards were killed.
Twelve convicts were hanged, in a couple of batches, and Norfolk Island was back to normal. But Maconochie's pioneering
performance was recognized in Victorian England as a very
worthy effort, and elements of his New System were soon introduced in the prisons of England and Ireland. In a pamphlet
written nine years before his death, the reformer argued on:

"It may be said that I overlooked, or even sacrificed, the
great object of punishment for which the prisoners were sent
to the island, but, as I conceive it, not so. What I really did spare
was the unnecessary humiliation which it is the fashion to impose on prisoners. This crushes the weak, unnecessarily irritates
the strong, indisposes all to submission and reform, and is, in
truth, neither intended by the law, nor consistent with the pro-
fessions made by lawyers while framing it."

In the young United States of America, by contrast, the
prison was first regarded as an instrument of humanitarianism.
The new word was "penitentiary." The prisoners were not to
be maltreated. There was food, light, clothing, exercise, ventilation, religious instruction, all that John Howard would wish
for this most helpful of new nations. The Quaker influence was
to predominate—and the Quakers were merciful folk who had
survived more than their share of physical violence. After 1776,
the Quakers were instrumental in founding "The Philadelphia

Society for Alleviating the Miseries of Public Prisons." Along with civic leaders such as Benjamin Franklin, Benjamin Rush and William Bradford, they set forth a body of principles of justice for America:

> Our obligations are not cancelled by the crimes of the guilty.
>
> We must extend compassion to the guilty.
>
> Undue suffering must be prevented.
>
> The links which bind the human family together must under all circumstances be preserved unbroken—there must be no criminal class.
>
> Such punishments may be devised as will restore them to virtue and happiness.

The new Pennsylvania state legislature had so much respect for these men that they did away with the whipping post and substituted fines and imprisonment. The legislature also permitted the Society to take over part of the old Walnut Street jail for experiments in prison reform. There, the Society decreed that sermons would be preached in prison, and the guards would be deprived of their clubs and canes "for fear that for trifling provocations they might be induced to beat a criminal."

When prisoners committed offenses they were "spoken to" by the prison officers but there were no harsh words to "damp the spirit of, or expose, the prisoners," and, at worst, they were put in solitary confinement. Morale soon went up to the extent that women prisoners, whose bed linen was now changed twice each week, introduced a rule of their own—the floors were to be kept scrubbed to an immaculate whiteness, and anyone who spat on the floor would be fined.

In Philadelphia, according to Cabel Lownes, the whole problem of crime suddenly appeared to have been solved. "Our streets meet with no interruption from those characters that formerly rendered it dangerous to walk out of an evening. Our houses, stores and vessels, so perpetually disturbed and robbed, no longer experience these alarming evils. There have been but two instances of burglary in this city and county for near two years. Pickpockets, formerly such a pest, are now unknown. . . . Out of near 200 persons pardoned by the governor, only four have been recommitted. If the discharged prisoners have returned to their old courses, they have chosen the risk of being hanged in other states rather than encounter the certainty of the penitentiary in this."

And although some critics of the Walnut Street jail complained that the prisoners of the Quakers must have been hypnotized or intimidated, no less an authority than the French visitor La Rochefoucauld denied it. He wrote: "Recall Dr. Hunter, of York, in England, who of all other physicians has cured most lunatics, by striking off their chains and leading them back to gentleness and reason. No one need be shocked by the comparison of fools and criminals."

The Walnut Street experiment was ahead of its time, however, and it was doomed to fail. The prison house was overcrowded, the officers were often incompetent, the administration of the place broke down to the point that reform seemed akin to lack of discipline. The state built two new prisons, and in the second of these, Cherry Hill, the obverse side of the Quaker tradition was put to prey on prisoners' minds. There was to be no violence, but there would also be no disorder. The penitentiary was to become the place of remorse in which men would have no alternative but to reflect upon their crimes. As one Quaker put it: "Let them walk their gloomy abodes, and commune with their corrupt hearts and guilty consciences in silence."

The new arrival at Cherry Hill in the 1830's was brought before the medical officer, a great grandson of Franklin. He was examined, bathed, and given a prison uniform. Then his eyes were blindfolded and he was led into the rotunda, where the rules were read to him by the superintendent. Still blindfolded, he was led to his cell, where the cloth was removed from his eyes. There he found himself in a room less than twelve feet long and eight feet wide. If he was installed on the ground floor, he looked out into a small courtyard of nearly the same dimensions.

In this place, the new prisoner lived out all of his sentence, year after year, even for life. He saw no other part of the prison, nor any other prisoner. He received no mail, no visitors. The guard who brought his food was not permitted to utter a word. The prisoner would be visited by prison officers known as "morals instructors" and he was encouraged to discuss his progress in "redemption." He worked in his cell if he wanted to, and this was taken as a good sign. The authorities would even set up small machines on which he could spin, weave, or make shoes. There was no coercion to work, however: if he chose, the prisoner communed with his soul in idleness.

Cherry Hill in its time was a model to many—a new concept in penal reform in which several prisoners even memorized most of the Bible. It was an example, according to Zephaniah Swift, of benevolence in the treatment of prisoners. It was praised by Tocqueville and it was copied in Europe. Charles Dickens damned Cherry Hill as "torture" and "agony" and "dreadful punishment prolonged," however, and over the years a high percentage of Cherry Hill's inmates went mad.

The second great prison concept in the United States was pioneered in New York State. Between 1821 and 1823, even before the founding of Cherry Hill, New York tested the principle of absolute solitary confinement but concluded, "To make any impression upon convicts there must be suffering." So New York built the largest penitentiaries in the country and began a reign of terror. The new element was that the whole prison population would have to work to turn out products for state profit. The traditional element was the return to the lash. And although the Pennsylvania experiments were tested for thirty more years in New Jersey, Maine, Maryland, Massachusetts, and Rhode Island, it was the New York system that set the pattern for the nation.

New York constructed the Auburn Penitentiary, virtually a prison within a prison, in which cells were built in rows, back to back, tier upon tier, the doors opening on to corridors and galleries. In Auburn's "congregate system," the prisoners were isolated in their cells at night, but worked together in great halls by day, compulsorily, in total silence. They were marched to and fro from work in military order, one hand on the shoulder of the man in front, their heads turned in the direction of the guards. Discipline was administered by Auburn's notorious Captain Lynds. The punishment was almost always flogging— for speaking, for lifting eyes up from work, for watching other men flogged, for the sane and insane alike.

Captain Lynds dominated the prison so completely that in 1825 he even offered to build the new Sing Sing Penitentiary with his inmate labor. Lynds brought them down the Hudson in freight vessels, each man shackled by one leg, and he started them to work that very day. By nightfall they had built a temporary shelter, a cookhouse and a blacksmith's and carpenter's shops. Through the summer, they built sixty small cells. Lynds then brought in more prisoners to quarry stone, haul the carts, and build the prison. Three years later Lynds had completed Sing Sing, and the nation applauded his virtuoso performance.

Because the New York system was intended to impress the whole citizenry, the prison officials invited thousands to visit Auburn and charged modest admission fees. The visitors stared down through small windows in the workshop walls, but the prisoners were not allowed to look up. The visitors often included wives, children, and friends of the men in Auburn making sure all was well. For the state, Auburn was a profitable as well as a deterrent attraction. In 1830, the prison listed receipts totaling fifteen hundred dollars from the conducted tours.

Harsh imprisonment spread to Maine, where prisoners were

confined in pits, sunken in the ground, entered by a two-foot hole in the roofs. The men remained in their pits, without heat, without light, without work, until the state switched to the congregate labor system. In New Hampshire, the state hired out its prisoners to work for private businessmen, who paid for prison labor cash on the barrelhead. In Ohio, prisoners were put to work, four men per call, in a kind of cottage industry program, but Ohio soon turned to the congregate system. Connecticut, which had located its first prison eighty feet below ground in an abandoned copper mine, opened a new prison at Wethersfield on the congregate plan. Then the wardens at Wethersfield stopped flogging the prisoners excessively, and production went up.

The western states set up their prisons as if cruelty was the point of punishment. In California, the grim story of the American penitentiary reached its lowest levels. In San Quentin, men were tied stark naked to ladders and whipped into insensibility. Prisoners were jetted with spouts of water played point-blank on their faces until blood poured from their ears. At Folsom, men were hung from a tackle known as "the derrick," their toes barely touching a floor that had been strewn with chloride of lime. San Quentin added "the tombs" for troublesome prisoners, in which men were confined in solid sheet-iron cells six-feet-by-four. Folsom tied up sane men in straight jackets and guards kicked and rolled them around.

Not long after the Civil War, the country seemed to agree that prison atrocities ought to be checked. In 1870, Ohio's Governor Rutherford B. Hayes, later President of the United States, invited 130 delegates from 24 states and several foreign countries to a National Prison Congress in Cincinnati. The congress was the brainchild of Enoch Cobb Wines, head of the New York Prison Association, and it reflected the ideas of Louis Dwight, a "pulpit reformer," and the practical gains achieved by the wardens of Wethersfield, Connecticut. Above all, the congress was a form of legacy from the illustrious

Captain Maconochie of Norfolk Island, whose New System of rehabilitation had by now been widely applied by Sir William Crofton in Ireland. The success of Maconochie-type programs was the topic of the hour and the touch of practicality at Cincinnati.

The man who moved to the forefront of the National Prison Congress was Zebulon Brockway, a professional prison administrator, forty-three years old, with a massive beard that was already turning white. Brockway was the warden of the Detroit house of correction and he was highly regarded for his ability to run profitable industries. He had persuaded friends in the city to offer jobs to discharged men with good records, and he had agitated among lawyers for the indeterminate sentence.

At Cincinnati, Brockway drafted the ideals of the "golden age of prison reform" into proposals. His celebrated address to the delegates, entitled "Ideal for a True Prison System for a State," advocated the establishment of reception centers in which incorrigible prisoners could be set aside. The overwhelming majority of the prisoners would then be sent to reformatories to serve indeterminate sentences, and would be released when they had accumulated enough "marks" for good behavior (Maconochie). They would also enter into formal schedules of academic and vocational training. Brockway said afterward that he felt strengthened during his address by "a mysterious, almighty and spiritual force," but his professionalism won the day. The congress adopted a declaration of purpose—rehabilitation, indeterminate sentences, marks for good behavior, education for all prisoners—both vocational and academic—no more brutal treatment, even "cultivation of the inmate's self-respect."

Seven years later, the New York state legislature invested the then phenomenal sum of $1,500,000 for a reformatory at Elmira where Brockway's ideas could be tested. Elmira was designed for young first offenders, but it was soon opened to all ages. There, Brockway grouped the men into three classes. New arrivals were admitted to the middle class, and were promoted or demoted in time according to their performance; after six months in the first class they were considered eligible for release "on parole." Emphasis was placed on academic and vocational classes, and Elmira soon boasted a library of several thousand books. There was no "barbarous treatment" and the familiar striped prison clothing was done away with. Brockway set up a "creative recreation" program with a gymnasium, athletic fields, a bank, and a glee club, and he insisted that religious instruction at Elmira be "adapted to the hereditary, habitual and preferable denominational predilection of the individual prisoners." Prison products were sold on the open market.

During the 1880's, however, all prisons in the United States came under a new form of pressure when the rising trades union movement argued against unfair competition by prison labor. But when the New York state legislature prohibited private contract work, Brockway devised new ways to rehabilitate his prisoners. He dressed them in smart, military-type uniforms, conducted tactical training exercises, and awarded officers' "commissions" to his best men. All this continued to work wonders.

In his final years at Elmira, Brockway was criticized for laxity and mismanagement, but he won important points when the state enacted the indeterminate sentence for selected offenders and permitted the resumption of manufacture of prison goods for sale to governmental agencies. On the last day of the nineteenth century, Brockway retired.

Before moving on to the story of our creation of the federal Bureau of Prisons, I will touch on the life of one more reformer who inspired me.

Thomas Mott Osborne, born in the shadow of the prison at Auburn in 1859, was what today we would call a prison buff. He was a prominent businessman, twice mayor of Auburn, who read and learned everything available about the evolution of prisons. He said, "What strikes us as obsolete today represents what was once a reform of an earlier maladjustment."

Osborne started a nationwide controversy by his organization of a system of self-government for prisoners. He had come to believe during his many years as trustee of the George Junior Republic, at Freeville, New York, that delinquent boys treated as "citizens and entrusted with the administration of their own country" would act with a heightened sense of responsibility. In 1913 he was appointed chairman of the New York state commission for prison reform and, believing he ought to meet the prisoners, he faked the identity of "Tom Brown," put on a prison uniform, and spent a week as a convict in Auburn. There he asked a man what could be done, for example, to brighten the dreary prison on Sundays. "Perhaps more walks in the yard?" When he was told that guards would not give up their Sundays off to watch the prisoners in the yard, Osborne asked, "You don't suppose the men could be trusted to walk by themselves, do you?" The prisoner said, "Why not. I tell you the big majority in here will be square if you give them the chance."

Osborne asked if there would be trouble if the prisoners were allowed to administer more of their privileges. There would be none, his companion said, and if a few "dirty degenerates" tried it, "we'd take care of them." So Osborne evolved a plan for a Good Conduct League, in which model prisoners would actually take over much of the running of the penitentiary.

Not long afterward "Tom Brown" made what must have been a dramatic reappearance at Auburn. At one Sunday morning chapel, he identified himself as the prison reform commissioner, and he asked if the men would cooperate with a Good Conduct League. There was a shout of approval. So Osborne set up a body of fifty delegates, elected by the prisoners on the basis of representation of the several workshops, and even a court of five "judges" chosen by the delegates. When he handed over the management of the workshops and a voice in prison discipline to the Good Conduct League there was a national uproar. But when he was moved to the wardenship of New York's other large prison, Sing Sing, Osborne coolly introduced what he now termed the Mutual Welfare League and he extended its authority over the vocational and recreational program.

Osborne's enemies charged that the Mutual Welfare League, for all its high idealism, was simply not imprisonment. He was undermining the intent of the courts, not to mention society, to punish criminals and to deter crime. Furthermore, he was beginning to abdicate control of the institution. One of his critics summed up that "the cause of prison reform is suffering from excess." Perhaps so—but at the time when Osborne was finally brought up for departmental hearings on charges of mismanagement, his league was engaged in a new campaign to wipe out the use of narcotics at Sing Sing.

In the hearings, Osborne was cleared of wrongdoing, but his power was broken and he decided to resign. The Mutual Welfare League collapsed and Osborne was left to proclaim to the next generation, "The League still lives—in the hearts of thousands of men who have felt its uplifting influence." In practical terms, however, the great wave of prison reform that had rolled out of Cincinnati since 1870 was checked.

VI

NO MORE NIGHTSTICKS, NO MORE LOCKSTEP, NO MORE CLOSE CONFINEMENT OF WOMEN

During my investigation of prison work for the Bureau of Efficiency in the mid-1920's, I was sitting on a bench at the bus stop outside the unfinished façade of the federal penitentiary at Leavenworth, Kansas. It had been a hot, tiring summer day, spent trudging around half-finished cellblocks, makeshift workshops, an abandoned brick kiln and storage rooms in and out of which prisoners darted in their pathetic efforts to appear to be busy. I reflected as I waited for the bus that the prison reforms of the present, as of the past, were all too often accomplished amid the drudgery of detail. Then, a short man with graying hair, dressed in the blue cotton pants and chambray shirt worn by prisoners, sat down on the bench beside me. I recognized him as a trustie returning to the penitentiary after finishing his day's work in a prison officer's home.

The man struck up a conversation. He began by saying that the Leavenworth grapevine had passed the word who I was and what I was doing, and what my general intentions were. He wanted me to know I had the good wishes and high hopes of the prisoners. When he asked me if I read *The New Era*, the Leavenworth prison newspaper, I realized I was talking to its editor, Dr. Frederick Cook, the North Pole explorer who had been convicted of using the mails to defraud in the sale of oil leases. Cook pointed to the unfinished dome of the penitentiary, then second in size in the country only to the U.S. Capitol dome in Washington. Would another generation pass, Cook asked, before we accepted the fact that our prison system was as far from reality as that preposterous dome? Cook was right: nothing I had seen at Leavenworth could even remotely be termed rehabilitative.

When I visited the second large federal penitentiary, at Atlanta, I found nothing was being done to help the thirty-five hundred prohibition act violators, drug addicts, counterfeiters, and mail fraudsters who were housed with major criminals in basement dormitories, improvised warehouses, and tents in the yard. Atlanta reminded me of what I had read about Andersonville, the infamous Civil War prison camp in Georgia in which fifteen hundred Union prisoners of war had died of disease or had been shot by the Confederate guards. At Atlanta, one prisoner had recently been reprimanded and listed in the prison logbook for picking his teeth. A second man had been sentenced to severe loss of privileges for dragging his feet while exercising. A third was given five days in "the hole" for throwing a Bible out of his cell. A fourth was handcuffed to his cell door for sixteen hours for laughing loudly on his way out of the mess hall after supper.

The federal penitentiary was a paradise compared to the state facilities, however, and our men considered themselves fortunate. This was the heyday of the chain gang in Georgia, when men in striped suits and shackles worked on the public highways, slept in cage wagons, and were locked in sweatboxes in the broiling sun. One hideous incident came to my attention at this time: some chain gang men who were caught planning an escape were forced to shake hands with a corpse shot in an escape attempt.

In some respects, life in Atlanta had its moments for a favored few, and there had been several scandals. The sale of paroles had been alleged, petty graft was rampant, and narcotics were in evident use. VIP prisoners were even seen in Atlanta night-clubs in the company of prison officials, and Mrs. Mabel Wille-brandt, a formidable assistant attorney general in the Coolidge administration, determined to look into things.

She sent an undercover agent of the then-fledgling Federal Bureau of Investigation into the penitentiary in the guise of a new inmate, and this turned out to be the joke of the year at Atlanta. Wardens, guards, and prisoners laughed at "the fool woman" and the FBI. The warden speedily identified the agent and put him in solitary confinement, and when Mrs. Wille-brandt found out what had happened, and ordered the warden to release the man, the warden adamantly refused. The agent had been formally and legally committed to a federal peni-tentiary, the warden said, and could not be released until the commitment was just as formally set aside. This took a little time.

The Justice Department, thus challenged, probed Atlanta publicly and thoroughly. The department also asked for the views of the Bureau of Efficiency on the goals, treatment, methods, and work policies of all of the federal prisons. The department was ready to terminate the state of affairs in which the prisons were answerable only to their own wardens, and in which Washington had minimal powers.

At the conclusion of my months of tours for the Bureau of Efficiency, I submitted a lengthy report, from which I quote in some detail because it was destined to mark a turning point.

The national government has never given adequate attention to its prison problem.

Perhaps the neglect of the national government is the reflection of the public mind.

Naturally, the social outcast is the last to receive attention.

At no time, however, has interest in penology been greater than it is today. Crime commissions, prison reform associations and legislative committees are busy overhauling and improving existing machinery. Attention so far has been devoted to the states, the federal government probably being allowed to escape because heretofore the number of men who transgressed U.S. statutes were relatively few in number.

But this neglect cannot long continue. The breaking point has about been reached. Something must be done without further postponement.

There is no need, however, for alarm, hysteria and blindly plunging ahead without thought or consideration of the problem as a whole. We have yet time to survey the field, formulate a policy, and evolve a co-ordinated and homogeneous federal correctional scheme.

In the report I detailed the history of the federal prisons in a country made up of states. Not until 1891 did Congress authorize the purchase of sites for the erection of three federal prisons, directing the transfer of the military prison at Fort Leavenworth, Kansas, to the Justice Department for the housing of civilian prisoners. In 1896, the construction of the walled Leavenworth Penitentiary began. Subsequently, Atlanta and an abandoned marshals' jail on McNeil Island in Puget Sound, Washington, were brought into the federal system. This organization was managed by a superintendent of prisons in Washington, with a staff of about a dozen clerks, bookkeepers, and inspectors. The wardens in charge of the prisons were political appointees of local U.S. senators, and were answerable, in effect, to them.

The main body of the report I devoted to a study of the shocking conditions in the prisons. I also considered the problems of juvenile delinquency, narcotics addiction, insane prisoners, repeat offenders, and the plight of federal prisoners in abominable local jails, especially in the southern states.

Then I made recommendations for major changes. I called for the establishment of the first federal prison bureau in our history, an organization to be set up within the Justice Department, with full powers to control the federal prisons. The first business of the new bureau would be to humanize prison life and to set an example to reformers in the states. I proposed that we should build three new penitentiaries and experimental-type institutions, also two new "narcotics farms" in which addicts could be treated separately from the rest of the prison population. All of this new system ought to be keyed, in the language of the statute, to a plan of rehabilitation. The theme would be "the individualized discipline, care and treatment of prisoners."

This was some going for a young investigator of the Bureau of Efficiency, I realized, and I concluded my report on a modest note. "It is to be hoped," I wrote, "that the foregoing limping and halting discussion will be of some help in understanding the problem, will afford a basis for crystallizing thought, and cause at least a few to devote passing attention to the human scrap heap."

In a second report, I urged more specifically that the emphasis of prison reform ought to be placed on work. This would involve an orderly development not only of prison workshops but also of prison industries. Around work schedules, a curriculum of vocational and academic education could be planned.

Not long afterward, I received a phone call from Sanford Bates, the celebrated prison administrator who had conducted notable reforms within the Massachusetts system. Bates was enthusiastic about my report, and he said it was a promising working paper for changes that could be enacted. President

Hoover had asked his attorney general, William D. Mitchell, to find ways of overhauling the federal prisons and Bates had been requested by the President to take charge of whatever new institutions emerged. Bates asked me if I would like to join him at the Justice Department and help him put my own report into effect. Then and there I accepted.

My assignment under Bates was to help write the legislative proposals for prison reform that Hoover would send to Congress. The first bill was the organic act that would set up the new federal Bureau of Prisons. I spelled out the organization of the bureau, and defined the mission. My second bill was the authorization of industries in the federal prisons—and this was a much tougher problem. So as to ensure markets for our products, I added a "compulsory purchase" clause that would require federal agencies to buy our goods. I knew I was inviting not only the hostility of the trade unions, but also that of the government agencies, which might be expected to resist any encroachment upon their freedom to purchase what and where they choose.

My strategy in wording the legislation was to tie the industries program and the compulsory purchase clause to a broad statement of the purpose of prison reform. President Hoover was thereby enabled to commit himself. He threw his prestige behind us and ordered his cabinet members to abandon their opposition to the compulsory purchase clause. Without undue delay, the prison bureau was created and the prison industries got under way.

Our successes in Congress led us to propose further legislation. We obtained authority to build two new prisons and a home for mentally ill prisoners. We established a full-time federal board of parole, and expanded the use of probation in federal cases. We also won congressional approval for a significant change in the role of the U.S. Public Health Service. When we invited it to administer medical and psychiatric care in the federal prisons, we were awarding the P.H.S. its first mission beyond the care of Coast Guardsmen and the management of quarantine at the ports. From this new start, the P.H.S. extended its responsibility widely and today it is involved in struggles to eradicate almost all forms of disease in the nation and abroad.

These were perhaps the most exciting days of my life. Preoccupied though we all were in the detail of our legal work, we understood the historical meaning of our accomplishments. President Hoover was a great leader. It seems absurd, today, that so many look back on the Hoover administration as a sort of vacuum that preceded the New Deal, when in fact it was a time of social progress in the midst of economic setbacks.

Sanford Bates's contribution was immense. He took his stand, as he once told me, on the assumption that either our social structure is hopelessly maladjusted or there must be causes that can be ascertained for the incidence of crime. He believed criminality could be cured in medical fashion and that punishment of criminals was out of date. Bates confidently took on all the early battles—funds were short and the country was heading into the Depression; judges, police officials, newspaper editors were campaigning against the "coddling" of criminals; prison wardens and guards usually thought that prison reform was "the bunk" and continued to believe in "the strap."

President Franklin D. Roosevelt, moving into the White House in 1933, ratified Hoover's charters for prison reform and he ordered his attorney general, Homer S. Cummings, to press them diligently. Contrary to general expectation, and to everyone's relief, Roosevelt reappointed Sanford Bates, though a Republican, as director of the federal Bureau of Prisons. FDR also reappointed three assistant directors and reaffirmed their responsibilities. Austin H. McCormick was in charge of academic and vocational training and the formulation of prison discipline reforms. William T. Hammack administered fiscal affairs and the recruitment and training of a new career service for prison personnel. I was the third assistant director, with the responsibility for the management of the prison industries. To all of us, President Roosevelt said one day: "To no other institutions of learning in the world do so many post-graduates return for advanced instruction as they do to the prisons—those colleges of crime—which a still unenlightened civilization has erected for quite a different purpose." He was to be our second inspirational chief.

The decisive engagement of prison reform in the New Deal years now broke out on my front. Organized labor, in the depths of the Depression, struck back at the prison industries and won swift legislative advantages. In 1934, the Hawes-Cooper Act divested prison-made goods of their status in interstate commerce. This gave the states the authority to stop our products at their state lines. In 1935, the Ashurst-Sumners Act prohibited transportation companies from accepting prison goods for shipment into any state in violation of that state's laws. Most of the states dropped the other shoe—and prohibited entry. All this imposed great hardship upon us, and, in an endeavor to awaken public opinion, I wrote:

"Most American state prisons are now merely vast, idle houses filled with a horde of despairing, discouraged, disgruntled men, milling aimlessly about an overcrowded prison yard. Out of the 160,000 men in prisons in this country today, less than 20,000 have any kind of employment other than time-wasting and energy-consuming tasks connected with the maintenance of the institution in which they are incarcerated. This is a grim, deplorable story."

Nor was this hyperbole: the Depression had struck a terrible blow to our hopes and aspirations. While some thirty per cent of our countrymen were out of work, more than eighty per cent of our prisoners had been deprived of any form of constructive, industrial occupation. Some of the more ingenious wardens were devising new ways of keeping their men busy. One warden put a man to work maintaining an electric motor that needed a drop of oil a day. Another assigned a prisoner to keeping salt shakers in straight lines down the rows of tables in the mess hall. Small wonder we were plagued during the Depression by outbreaks of minor, meaningless prison riots.

Undaunted by the misery in the prisons, our congressional adversaries now found a way to undermine the compulsory purchase clause of the Hoover reform legislation. No less a social reformer than Representative Fiorello LaGuardia of New York, responsive to chambers of commerce and trade unions, offered an amendment to one of our appropriations bills denying us funds for the production of office furniture and brushes for sale to government agencies. The LaGuardia amendment became law and part of our industries program was ruined. In this critical situation, Mrs. Franklin D. Roosevelt came to our assistance. She had decided to make prison reform one of her personal areas of interest in the New Deal and, after conferring with Sanford Bates and me about the LaGuardia problem, she intervened. Mrs. Roosevelt took up the issue with her husband and, apparently, sent a memorandum pressing him to find ways to demolish the LaGuardia amendment. The President's office asked us to come up with a plausible formula.

It now occurred to me that we might be able to utilize a bureaucratic device that had proven effective in other areas of the New Deal. I proposed the formation of a new government corporation, not unlike the Reconstruction Finance Corporation, to manage prison industries. The corporation would have its own capital and operating funds, and its own board of directors, and would work outside the laws controlling government agencies. We would not need congressional approval of funds for making office furniture and brushes. This plan, drafted into a statute, was sent to President Roosevelt.

In due course, and probably after the prodding of his wife, Roosevelt called Bates and me to his office. There we found William Green, president of the American Federation of Labor, and several other trade union leaders. Roosevelt explained to Green the purpose of the proposed prison industries corporation and the broader importance of rehabilitation, and asked for Green's cooperation. Green asked for time to consider but Roosevelt was impatient. He suggested that Green and his friends go out to the anteroom to talk it over while he covered some other prison business with Bates and me. Five minutes later, Green returned and said he would be glad to cooperate (a political debt Roosevelt doubtless repaid in some other coin). We had won. No opposition was raised against the Federal Prison Industries, Inc., in its passage through Congress. Bates was named president. Representatives of business, labor, and consumers and retailers, also farmers, were elected to the board of directors. I was appointed commissioner of prison industries with operational responsibility.

The corporation began to roll. For governmental markets, we made mail bags, shirts, blouses, shoes, gloves, mats, brooms, brushes, hardware, desks, chairs, beds, metal furniture, and light industrial products. I defined the controlling philosophy: "Primary emphasis must be placed upon work which will train inmates in skills likely to provide them with adequate livelihood upon release."

Two years after its inception in 1937, Federal Prison Industries sold $3,777,000 in goods and services and made a profit of $567,698. We scarcely believed this could be done in a Depression year. We had a cotton textile mill at Atlanta, a shoe factory at Leavenworth, a garment facility at Alderson, brush factories at Alcatraz and Leavenworth, print shops at Atlanta and Leavenworth, and a modern machine, tool, and die shop at the El Reno reformatory in Oklahoma. By the beginning of World War II we were operating twenty-one separate small industries with an average daily employment of 3,421 men. Our annual sales grossed $5,500,000 and we began to plow back our profits into expanded vocational training courses. Some of the states, impressed by our success, extended their own prison work plans.

During World War II, our shops and factories were converted into small war plants. We made bomb fins, gun brushes, and a variety of armament and support goods. By 1941, almost ninety-five per cent of our output was for our defense effort, or for lend-lease to our allies. The prison work week went from forty to forty-eight hours per week and the men were paid overtime. In 1942 we increased our production fourfold over that of 1940. In 1943, we had forty-nine plants in operation. We even had an Airplane Mechanics School at the Chillicothe, Ohio, reformatory, and our graduates were in demand in the Air Corps and, after the war, in civilian airlines and aircraft companies.

Following a temporary cutback in sales after the war, Federal Prison Industries continued to expand until in 1964, the year of my retirement, sales reached nearly forty million dollars, with four million dollars paid into the U.S. Treasury in dividends and additional profits earmarked for more vocational training. Prisoners could earn as much as seventy-five dollars per month free and clear. They were learning useful trades that would help them after their release, were gaining in self-confidence, and were absorbing their prison experience. Outside the prisons, according to our records, the men who had learned good work habits in the industry and accumulated sizable savings were far less likely to become recidivists than those who did not cooperate in the program.

In 1937, I was appointed by Attorney General Cummings to succeed Sanford Bates as director of the Bureau of Prisons. Bates had been asked by former President Hoover to become director of the Boys Clubs of America and had accepted. President Roosevelt called me to his office and told me, at some length, about his own belief in prison reform and about his concern that our prisons were too cruel. He offered to do everything possible to help me correct these abuses, and, with FDR's engaging smile and warm handshake, I went off to my new duties.

Thus heartened and empowered, I resolved to make a drastic start. In a series of steps, I decided to extend the reforms commenced by Bates and to change the shape and style of imprisonment under federal jurisdiction. I felt the spirit of Howard and Maconochie, Brockway and Osborne would now inspire me. At my side, as always, was my wife, gently urging me on.

I struck first and hardest at what would now be called the "gut issue" of prison reform—brutality. In my first administrative order, I ruled that prison guards were no longer permitted to carry nightsticks, truncheons, or clubs. I knew that corporal punishment was not allowed in federal prisons but also that it was secretly practiced, and that the nightstick was in fact the symbol of punitive authority. I made it plain to all the wardens that there was to be no lashing, no use of the strap, no handcuffing men to the bars, no improper solitary confinement. When the guards were told by the wardens they could no longer carry their nightsticks, they resented it and their wives complained to their congressmen, but finally they realized I meant what I said and was willing to live or fall by it.

Next, I ordered that prisoners could no longer be punished by removal of good-conduct credits without approval by my office in Washington. I retained for my own office the right to pass on any infraction of prison discipline in which prisoners were to be denied important privileges.

The working relationship between the prison guards, most of whom were quite cooperative, and the prisoners improved as the mutual fear diminished. One Tennessee warden, on a tour of inspection of a federal prison, jokingly asked his guide: "O.K. I've seen all your showplaces. Now show me where you whip 'em." When the federal officer told the Tennessean there was no whipping in the prison, the visitor laughed. "You come work for me any time, boy," he said. "You know how to keep your mouth shut." In fact, the standard punishment was administrative segregation, known as "seg." Prisoners who were insolent, refused to work, or disobeyed orders were confined in isolated cells for several days. They were given the standard prison ration, and although they were not allowed to receive letters, they could write them and were allowed books and tobacco. If a prisoner was obstreperous here he was removed to punitive segregation where he was deprived of all privileges. The idea was to cool off offenders, and it worked for most.

Those of our critics who thought I was coddling convicts were soon brought up short by the manner in which we handled really serious violations. Time off for good behavior was something to be earned in federal prisons, but we never hesitated to take away the good-conduct credits of offenders who were assaultive or completely recalcitrant. When infractions of prison rules amounted to felonies, e.g., serious assault, rioting, homosexual attacks, we brought the men into the nearest federal court and charged them with the commission of offenses "on a federal reservation." They were liable to additional sentences, if convicted. With these powers to reduce or increase time spent in jail, in effect, we did not need the nightstick. Soon the prison wardens and guards realized that physical brutality was out of date.

With the issue of prison cruelty resolved in the federal system, my associates and I felt free to promulgate new administrative orders. The bureau ruled, for instance, that every prisoner should get a standard ration of five pounds of food per day, and a varied menu was introduced in the federal prisons. Cafeterias were installed to replace the hoary old food buckets. Mealtime silence, with its overtones of Cherry Hill and Auburn, was abolished, and the men were allowed to talk. We eliminated waiting in line at the cafeterias as far as we were able. We let the men walk to their meals at any time the mess hall was open and serving; no longer were they required to march in silently, and they were free to choose any four-man table instead of long benches. They could eat with whomever they chose. In the first of several moves to desegregate the federal prisons, we urged Negro and white prisoners to sit at meals together, work together, and share cells and dormitories.

Next, we expanded recreational facilities—baseball, football, volleyball, and indoor games such as table tennis. Our prison baseball leagues soon reached comparatively high standards. We supplied books, magazines, newspapers, radios, and, in time, television. There were libraries and reading rooms in which there was a rule of silence.

The grim screens and barriers, through which prisoners and their families had peered at one another during visiting hours, were torn down. We re-equipped the visiting rooms with sofas, tables, armchairs, and other furniture so that men and relatives could enjoy one another's company. When these changes were well received, I decided to lengthen visiting hours. Several of our wardens arranged outdoor visiting areas in which people could picnic together.

Mindful that men had once been locked in their cells "from sundown to sunup," I set back the hour for lights out, and scheduled vocational and academic activities in the evenings. And for prisoners who had demonstrated good behavior we assigned individual cubicles rather than open barracks and semi-private unlocked rooms.

President Roosevelt personally approved another symbolic change that reflected simple sense. In one of my early reports to Sanford Bates, I had remarked that "congestion in the federal prisons and other institutions makes it impossible to develop a satisfactory method of housing, classifying, employing or caring for federal prisons," and I recommended that we construct new prisons in which we would be able to develop individualized training. During the mid-1930's these new prisons included the medium-security penitentiary at Lewisburg, Pennsylvania, the medical center at Springfield, Missouri, correctional institutions at Milan, Michigan, and La Tuna, Texas, the reformatory at El Reno, Oklahoma, and, to handle the maximum-security criminals of the gangster era, Alcatraz.

In planning the Lewisburg Penitentiary, we agreed that all prisoners did not need cells, and we made architectural allowances for differences in prison behavior. Along with the architect, Alfred Hopkins, an admirer of gothic form, we came up with a design that included cells, dormitories, cubicles, and semi-private rooms.

We decided to build the traditional high walls around Lewisburg in a kind of reformers' rationale that it would make a greater degree of outdoor recreation possible. After I became director, however, I substituted double-chain link fences, saving a considerable amount of government money and winning the praises of the President. FDR told me he was convinced the physical form of institutions ought to reflect their ideals. It followed that we ought to move toward prisons without bars.

I was bold enough, or naïve enough, to jump into the controversy that raged then as now about the role of narcotics in our society. In the mid-1920's, when I entered government service, narcotics users amounted to one in one thousand of our population. Some two thousand federal prisoners were estimated to have taken drugs in one form or another, and in confinement, they tended to be troublemakers. They were white men for the most part, in their late twenties and early thirties, and they came from large cities. They made little or no attempt to rationalize their plight in psychological or social terms: they were simply mainline joy poppers, filled with self-pity, knowing no other way to obtain gratification, and they responded very poorly to such rehabilitative efforts as were then being made. A considerable percentage of these men came from well-off families, claiming they had become addicted following illness and an overgenerous prescription of morphine.

All this must seem very elementary in today's terms, when more than a thousand heroin addicts are convicted of various crimes in New York City every month, when much of a new generation is sampling marijuana in part in protest against almost everything. Nonetheless, it seemed to me in those days that we had a real problem on our hands. So I recommended to my superiors in the Justice Department the creation of a "farm" where narcotics offenders could be treated. The concept was that addicts were sick people who ought to be taken out of the prison populations. I was also concerned that the narcotics offenders in the prisons would slow down the new programs I wished to introduce and I wanted these men to be treated in the farms as a separate category.

Fortunately, my recommendations attracted the eye of Representative Stephen Porter, then chairman of the House Committee on Foreign Affairs. Porter was an authority on drugs who had attended several League of Nations conferences on narcotics control. He had read deeply in the history of "the evil flower," with its dramas of clipper ships beating up and down the China coast, the opium dens and the sleep of tranquillity, and the emergence in Sicily, Mexico, and the United States of incredible empires of crime. In frequent meetings, I briefed Porter about how federal prisoners managed to smuggle drugs into their cells in their clothing, in contraband packages, in hollowed-out textbooks and Bibles and, in one instance, in the cavity behind one man's glass eye. Porter said he would support the narcotics farm proposals, which were subsequently adopted by President Hoover and expanded by President Roosevelt. Thus we obtained before World War II a federal hospital for the treatment of our narcotics offenders at Lexington, Kentucky, and a public health service hospital at Fort Worth, Texas.

At the time, I believed we were making great strides in coping with the problem. We were taking our narcotics addicts out of federal prisons and were treating them with varying results. Meanwhile, the number of drug users brought to us appeared to decline. During World War II, when we were cut off from most of the overseas supply sources, narcotics convictions under federal jurisdiction fell to an all-time low. And although these moved upward again after the war, there was a second stabilization during the early Eisenhower years. But then the civil rights and youth revolutions brought an increase in the use of narcotics in the country that exceeded four hundred per cent—and soon we were virtually swamped. The percentage of

Negroes among federal narcotics prisoners increased from thirteen per cent in 1946 to fifty-three per cent in 1957 and it has climbed much more steeply since then.

Yet, I still felt compelled to plead for perspective. In one year in which Negroes among our narcotics prisoners exceeded ninety per cent, I specifically ordered a complete investigation of all admission records and we could not trace a single commitment for drug violations by a Negro farmer from a southern state.

To the end of my career in the prison service, I opposed those of our citizens who wished to lock up drug addicts for life (they could not throw them into the sea), and I insisted that addiction was an illness to be treated in clinics, not prisons. I also said that "Segregation, residential or othewise, necessarily brings with it the animosities and prejudices that breed rebellion against the mores of the dominant white race. The true fight against narcotics has to be fought in the slums and in all of our moves against poverty and despair."

The fundamental change of my early years that loomed much more urgently was the basic reform of prison medicine. We have seen how Congress placed responsibility for the medical and psychiatric care of federal prisoners, at our urging, with the Public Health Service. This was to turn into a major effort that we had scarcely envisaged as our knowledge of the psychiatric factors of crime began to expand. Our first job was to concentrate on such rudimentary health problems as the medical examination of incoming prisoners. We could scarcely credit the poor condition of so many of our disadvantaged Americans —yaws, hookworm, dysentery, and most of the physical plagues of poverty we now associate with the undeveloped countries of Asia, Africa, and Latin America. Then dental condition of the men was appalling.

Therefore, we placed full-time medical officers at each institution. Incredibly, this had never been done before. We enlisted part-time specialists and consultants to help the prison doctors.

We brought trained medical orderlies into the institutions to replace the prisoners with a smattering of medical knowledge ("Doc") who had previously treated serious illnesses on their own. There were among our population many forgotten, under-nourished, malformed citizens of the Depression era that the Public Health Service now attempted to restore to health.

One of the doctors I met when I made my first study of Leavenworth had told me, "Bathing facilities for 3,200 men might be said not to exist. This leads to disaster from the health point of view. Superficial infections have been contracted as a result of insufficient bathing. There is also no way of knowing whether a man has been exposed to or is in the presence of one of the contagious diseases. During the year, we had some scattered cases of mumps. Fortunately, it was mumps rather than scarlet fever, diphtheria, or some other epidemic." And he added, "If trouble comes, our duty has been discharged and the blame may fall where it is due."

With the help of such dedicated public health doctors as Walter Treadway, Lawrence Kolb, Justin Fuller, Charles Smith, and Jack Mazur we immensely improved our medical service. In historical terms, we had scarcely begun to develop our classification system and casework programs, nor had we done much about probation and parole techniques, the equalization of sentences, prisons without bars, pre-release and work-release experiments, the integration of treatment of prisoners within the community, or the formulation of a national strategy against crime, all of which would form the theme of my later years in office. In the broad sweep of prison reform, however, we had very clearly come a very long way from the day I toured Ohio State Penitentiary with Warden Thomas and wondered despairingly whether anything could be changed.

VII

ALCATRAZ

Not long after I was appointed federal prison director, I made a tour of inspection of our maximum-security institution on Alcatraz Island in San Francisco Bay. Three years before, we had taken over an old Army disciplinary barracks, added more living space, built gun towers and gun galleries, and created a society of 364 criminals surrounded by swirling tidal waters that made escape impossible. Alcatraz was a tough, minimum-privilege prison meant to deter the racketeers and those who tried to emulate them. Also, as Attorney General Homer S. Cummings put it, Alcatraz took the strain off the rest of the federal system. Once the troublemakers and the escape-prone had been sent to Alcatraz, it would be possible to ease the regimentation and set a free climate in the mainland prisons.

In a sense, I was the talent scout for Alcatraz. One of my

jobs was to review the records of all the men in the various federal prisons and decide who would be sent to "the Rock." I also had to supervise the performance of the men on Alcatraz and help determine who was ready to be sent back to prisons on the mainland.

The desk set aside for me to interview prisoners on my first visit as director was located in a drafty, cheerless, half-lit corner of the main cellblock. It was just below, but out of earshot of, an elevated, barred walkway where a guard armed with an automatic rifle was pacing. A second guard patrolled the polished concrete main floor. The moment a prisoner who had asked to see me took his place at the other side of the desk, the guard trained his rifle on his chest. When I protested to Warden James Johnston that the men might not feel free to speak their minds, he explained that Alcatraz was unlike any other prison. These were the most desperate men in the world, he said, and they might regard it as an accomplishment to assault the prison director.

Al Capone was one of the first men brought out to see me. He wore a one-piece, high-collared coverall reminiscent of my fatigues in World War I. He had no prison pallor, and the famous scar was less noticeable than the marks on the faces of many other prisoners. He did not snarl, as most of the movies, books, and plays about him had led me to expect. He was the most prominent gangster of all time, but he was serving an eleven-year sentence only for income tax evasion. No one had ever been able to prove he had killed a man.

Capone had been sent to Alcatraz because he was too big a problem for our officers at Atlanta to handle. He behaved well enough at Atlanta, but he still comported himself as the king of crime. Everywhere he was accompanied by bodyguards. At his work assignment in the shoe shop he was surrounded by other prisoners seeking favors. During recreation periods he liked to play tennis, and he never had to wait in line for a game. If he wanted to play doubles, someone would quit a foursome

to make room. If he wanted to play singles, Capone would indicate the man he wanted to play with, and the other would
walk off the court. Capone expended his monthly ten dollars'
canteen allowance in the first moments of each month, and yet
he always seemed to have all the cigar and canteen supplies he
wanted. Only after we had transferred him to Alcatraz did we
find a tennis racket with a hollowed-out handle in which Capone
reputedly kept several thousand dollars at a time.

In his first year at Alcatraz, Capone was abruptly dethroned.
The guards were incorruptible and the other prisoners were
tough. We gave him the humble work assignment of mopping
floors, and soon he became known as "The Man With The
Mop." When Capone elbowed ahead one day to the front of
the line in the barber shop a tough young prisoner named Jimmy
Lucas, also waiting in line, told Capone to get back to the end.
Lucas, who feared no one, was in prison for hijacking a
gambling ship off the coast of California. When Capone looked
at Lucas in blank astonishment and made no move to go to the
rear Lucas grabbed a pair of scissors from the inmate barber
and jabbed Capone. It was a superficial wound from which
Capone walked away without attempting a comeback. Capone's
prestige at Alcatraz took a resounding setback from that moment.

Now Capone was before me, smiling ingratiatingly, telling
me the injustices to which he had been subjected. He was, he
said, the victim of a vicious and unjust sentence—the only man
ever sentenced to ten years for evading his income taxes and an
additional year for failure to file. Obviously, he said, the judge
had sent him to prison for a long term because of his reputation
and not for income tax evasion. Was that due process of law or
even-handed justice? he asked. "I'm not lily white," he told me,
"but most of the stuff the newspapers reported about me was
the bunk and they knew it." He protested that no law officer had
ever been able to prove a single crime against him. When I told
him he was by his own admission certainly guilty of cheating the

government out of its taxes and that he must have done more than sing loud in church to get all his money, he took another tack.

He began to talk about his life in Chicago and he depicted himself as a twentieth-century Robin Hood. He had, for instance, settled a newsboy's strike and gotten the Chicago *Tribune* back on the streets, he claimed, because he felt sorry for the newsboys. When the *Tribune* was being driven off Chicago's streets by Moses Annenberg's gang, which was heading the circulation drive of the Hearst newspapers, Al said he was called in to "settle" the matter. In the gang warfare that followed some five or six men were gunned down. When I asked him about this he said it was too long a story to go into— but he would be glad to tell me where I could check on how he had made sure that the hundred thousand dollars he had refused to accept for his "peacemaking" services had gone to a hospital of his choosing.

After casually mentioning the possibility of transfer back to the mainland, or at least a change in work assignment, Capone came to the point. He said he would give me exclusive rights to write a book about him and would tell me everything he knew about the gang wars. "I'll tell you who to see and where you can check on everything I say. It'll sell and I'll throw in the movie rights." Capone was offering me a bribe worth scores of thousands of dollars and he was shaken when I said that, in my position, I could not do it. "I'm not trying to bribe you," he insisted. "All I want is for people to know the facts."

This was the only time Capone requested an interview, and I never saw him again. In his new situation, he kept to himself, avoided the other prisoners, obeyed the prison regulations, and became in fact as well as in name "The Man With The Mop." Capone was also a serious venereal case, and despite everything we did with heavy metals, his health declined. Shortly before his release, he became talkative and euphoric and he waxed complimentary about the treatment he had received from the federal Bureau of Prisons. To one visitor, he vowed he would see to it that James V. Bennett was the next attorney general of the United States, perhaps, because I could not be bought. Capone died in Miami not long after his release.

I was almost as curious, that day in 1937, about the second man who took his place across the desk beneath the leveled Springfields of the guards. He was Joe Smith, the victim of a malicious infliction of excessive punishment by a federal judge, and one of our most serious behavior problems. He stole some letters from an apartment mailbox, was caught on the spot by postal inspectors, and it was his luck that one of the letters contained one thousand dollars in checks. When he pleaded guilty to the theft and cooperated with the government by testifying against a co-defendant, the judge nevertheless sentenced him to fifteen years imprisonment, even though he was a first offender.

Smith shouted impulsively at the judge, "I hope you're here when I get out," and the judge gave him five more years for contempt of court. Small wonder that Smith was violent in prison, breaking up the cell furniture, attacking the guards, screaming wild threats against the judge. After the judge died of natural causes Smith transferred his hostility to all federal officers, and we felt we had to move him to Alcatraz for safe keeping. But there he began to behave, perhaps because he realized we sympathized with him.

Smith started the interview with me by launching into another tirade against his judge. "He was asleep most of the time during the trial. I just blew my top." I calmed him down, and Smith apologized, and added his regrets for the trouble he had caused me. Was there anything he could do to put things right? he asked. I told Smith his best course would be to work for parole. "Without parole, you'll have to serve out your whole term, and there's nothing I can do about it." This would mean hard work, cooperation with the authorities, talks with the chaplain and psychiatrist, and an effort to become known as a model prisoner.

Then, I added, if the parole application was submitted, and turned down, I might be able to apply for executive clemency from the President. This turned out to be one of my more successful days in office, because Smith did exactly what I recommended. Apparently I had convinced Smith that not all federal law officers were vindictive and had given him a more favorable impression of the law. Smith obtained his transfer to the mainland and his parole when eligible. He still sends me a card at Christmas, telling me proudly about his job and fine family.

Always when I went to Alcatraz after that first day in 1937 it seemed to me that this was the place where the legend of the big house in the annals of crime would live the longest and die the hardest. Alcatraz was never without a sense of fantasy. The rock itself, standing in the cold and deathly currents, was not as bleak and barren as it seemed from off shore. Here and there flowers sprang unexpectedly from patches of earth brought over from the mainland, and shrubbery, even one or two trees, had been coaxed to grow. Roadside walls were draped with vines and one or two grassy spots softened the appearance of the crags. Warden Johnston's home on the peak of the rock was like the pilothouse of a ship at anchor in the bay, beneath the cottony clouds. At night, I would stand at the guest-room window and listen to the steel doors of the cellblocks clanging open and shut while the guards said to one another, as if they were at sea, "All's well." "All's well," or "O.K."—"O.K."

Not long after my interviews with Capone and Smith, I returned to Alcatraz to investigate reports of increasing tension at the prison. I had received anonymous letters from prison officers expressing their fear that a riot was about to break out, and the warden had written to say there were undercurrents of violence. Through the "snitch box," a mail drop I had installed for prisoners to send me their grievances direct, I had begun to receive threats. But when I arrived at Alcatraz, things seemed quiet enough. I spent the evening in Johnston's living room before a cheerful fire in the grate. Whenever a gust of wind blew down the chimney, scattering ashes in the hearth, a white-jacketed houseman entered the room noiselessly, swept the ashes back into the fireplace, and withdrew. He must have been watching all the time.

Then it began—a long, shrill shriek EEEEEEOOOOOOOWWWWWWW from the direction of the main cellblock. This was followed by yells from the other prisoners, "Pipe down!" "Dummy up!" "Knock it off!" and a chorus of boos and obscenities. The shrieking continued, but at spaced intervals. After every five minutes, EEEEEEEEEEOOOOOOOOOOOWWWWWWWWWWW, more shouting and cursing. In the silence of San Francisco Bay, the noise was deafening.

Warden Johnston quickly checked the source of the trouble and reported there was no sign of a riot. The shrieker was a man who had been in and out of prisons all his life, and who was now experimenting with a new technique for putting everyone's nerves on edge. The warden told me he could lock the man up in one of the dungeons in the basement, but he added with a sharp look at me, "I've been ordered not to do things like that." I said nothing and the warden did no more, and the prisoner shrieked at five-minute intervals until dawn.

The next morning I went down to breakfast, unsure of what to expect or of how deep the disaffection lay. The warden said he had just talked with the shrieking prisoner, who assured us he was not trying to start a riot, but wanted to force a congressional investigation of his imprisonment. The man apparently resented his mother's lack of interest in his plight. I was not certain of the over-all situation, however, and ordered a full-dress inspection of the whole prison.

Accompanied by guards, Johnston and I walked over to the prison buildings and entered the control room. This nerve center of Alcatraz was protected to waist height by $\frac{3}{8}$-inch steel and from waist height to the ceiling by $1\frac{1}{2}$-inch bulletproof glass. Inside were the annunciator panels and other communications devices through which we could listen in to any part of the prison, or speak to any of the guards on duty. There was a board of keys with each one numbered for accounting whenever it had to be moved, or replaced. There was also a sizable arsenal of rifles, revolvers, shotguns, hand grenades, tear gas, ammunition, and billy clubs.

The warden and I proceeded through a series of steel doors into the main cellblock. It was peaceful. The 250 men who lived there had finished their breakfast and were waiting for the bell that would signal the end of the count. The bell rang, the count was in order, and the tension was lessening perceptibly.

Somewhat more relaxed, we strolled down "Broadway," the main street of the cellblock, and we noted the names on the doors of the individual cells. They read like a roster of the VIPs of Chicago and other cities in the old days. Each cell was clean, and the beds were well made, toilet articles in the prescribed places, personal belongings in order. I noticed that the prisoners had a surprising number of books on their shelves and there were paintings on the walls. The men had done these on their recreation and vocational time, and some of the oils and watercolors were excellent. The man who followed Johnston as warden, Edward Swope, owed much of his success as an outstanding prison administrator to his unflagging determination to help the prisoners in his custody. He persuaded one of his friends on the mainland, the owner of Rickeys Restaurant, to hang the work of Alcatraz prisoners on the restaurant walls and sell a few, and this money helped the prisoners.

On this inspection tour Johnston and I walked into the main dining room—its tear gas instant-release mechanism all too visible in the ceilings—and into the kitchen, where the bakers and butchers were preparing the midday meal. The food at Alcatraz was always considered superior to that served in any other federal prison because there were fewer to cook for and we tried harder to please the many gourmets among the big-name population who appreciated highly-seasoned fare and expert cooking. Most prison riots, as a matter of fact, are triggered by poor food. But the warden and I could find no ground for complaint or signs of an impending riot. We concluded our inspection by touring the workshops, hospital, and library, and listened for a while to the prison orchestra rehearsing in the auditorium.

After lunch, we decided to hold a routine meeting of the classification committee in which we would review the cases of a few model prisoners and decide whether they were ready for transfer to the mainland. The first man had stolen a car at the age of thirteen, was an accomplice in a murder at the age of seventeen, and had been sent to Alcatraz for bad behavior. On the Rock, he had attempted to escape and had attacked an officer. But then he appeared to appreciate the futility of this approach, and became a cooperative prisoner. He began to read extensively and, to our astonishment, he wrote a commentary on Hegel and Schopenhauer, which he sent to me in Washington. We had already made a tentatively favorable judgment by letting him work in the prison kitchen, where there were knives available, and he had performed safely. All the signs were positive and we agreed to send him to a mainland penitentiary.

The second man was also ready for return. He was a bank robber who had fought a gun battle with FBI agents but, on the Rock, he had been obsessed with despair. He once sent a letter to me in Washington: "The years in prison have more than served to impress upon me the utter uselessness of the acts which resulted in my imprisonment. And I suppose that 'prison is the only safe medium through which a cure for criminality can be sought.' But my conduct and never-ending effort for self-improvement have been predicated on a constant hope of a normal worth-while way of life." We decided to send him to another penitentiary, and he did not let us down.

After the classification committee meeting, I held some impromptu interviews with men who asked for changes in work assignments or sought openings in academic and vocational programs, and with others who had some grievances. One prisoner wanted the rules relaxed so he could present to the secretary of the Navy a new device that he considered suitable for anti-submarine warfare. I arranged this, and later, to my amazement, I was informed that it was a most useful and innovative technique they intended to adopt in part. Another wanted me to send an apology to the FBI agents who had arrested him: he had accused the FBI men of stealing his money and he was sorry for questioning their integrity.

The final interview of this day stayed in my mind for several reasons. The prisoner, whom I shall call Ted Mitchell, was serving a thirty-year sentence for counterfeiting. I had watched his progress with considerable interest. Mitchell and an accomplice had burglarized an engraving company and later, at gunpoint, they had forced an expert engraver to make a plate for counterfeiting ten-dollar bills. They broke into a printing plant, made up 120 of the bills, and put them in circulation. When arrested and taken into custody, Mitchell escaped and attempted to swim away across a river, but he was caught. He was an audacious and aggressive individual and, when I looked into his record, I found he had taken and passed the entrance examination for the U.S. Military Academy at West Point. He had lost the appointment when a previous instance of juvenile delinquency came to light.

Mitchell was sent to Leavenworth, where he hatched a plot to seize my successor as the head of the Federal Prison Industries, Alfred H. Connor, who had been planning a tour of inspection. The scheme was to use Connor as a shield while several prisoners fought their way out. Mitchell had even manufactured a crude and workable gun. When our informants in Leavenworth told us about the plot, we moved Mitchell to Alcatraz and took away his good-conduct credits.

Mitchell seemed poised, a man still in his thirties and in excellent health. "Two things, Mr. Bennett," he began. The first was predictable: he had been behaving well and wanted transfer to the mainland. I declined. "You've been pretty ready to use a gun in the past. Now you can earn your way out." His second idea was for federal prisoners to volunteer for arduous duties in the U.S. Trust Territories in the Pacific. Mitchell had done his homework, and he documented the maladministration of the territories, and suggested tasks that prisoners might undertake for the benefit of the islanders. Although the plan could not be implemented, it had merit.

Then Mitchell wanted to discuss some of my early writings on prison reform. He said, "You know, Mr. Bennett, there are three reasons why men are sent to prison. For punishment, for rehabilitation, and to protect the public. Sometimes, I think the last two are lost sight of in giving sentences. If a man spends three, or five, or ten years away from his family and friends, under fair but repressive treatment, shut up inside a cell, deprived of all the graces of normal living, and forced to follow a monotonous routine, isn't that too much? I think most prisoners would say no to prison reform—they'd say 'Go on, make the prisons tough, make them really rough, even brutal, but make the sentence short and get it over with.' Nobody would think of whipping a man, day after day, month after month, for the same offense. But years of imprisonment are worse."

Mitchell made his comeback and was eventually sent back to Leavenworth. There he made another good adjustment and was paroled. He is now in charge of production for a successful small business, saves his money, and cherishes responsible citizenship.

That day, I took Mitchell's warning seriously, if only because I had recently received through the "snitch box" another letter about the scarcely tolerated pressures of maximum-security imprisonment. It was from George "Machine Gun" Kelly, the leader of the notorious gang that had once terrorized the southwest and robbed numerous banks. Kelly wrote me: "Maybe you have asked yourself how can a man of even ordinary intelligence put up with this kind of life at Alcatraz. What is this life of mine like? To begin with, these five words seem written in fire on the walls of my cell—NOTHING CAN BE WORTH THIS. No one knows what it is like to suffer from the intellectual apathy, the pernicious mental scurvy, that comes of long privation of all that makes life real. A prisoner cannot help be haunted by a vision of life as it used to be and at such times I pay, with a sense of delicious melancholy, my tribute to life as it once was."

Machine Gun Kelly was eventually sent to Leavenworth, where he died of a heart attack.

The pressure cooker of maximum-security imprisonment at Alcatraz finally exploded at 6:10 P.M., May 2, 1946—3:10 P.M. San Francisco time. A teletype clattered in my office in the capital:

ALCATRAZ. URGENT. PRISONER LOOSE IN CELL-
HOUSE WITH GUN. SITUATION SERIOUS. MORE LATER.
STAND BY.

How had the prisoner obtained the gun? Every visitor to the island was scanned by a metals detector. Every package received on the island was searched. Every weapon used by the prison officers was inspected and accounted for at every change of shift. The only access to the gun gallery was from a catwalk outside the building, and how could a prisoner climb up there? Within ten minutes, there was another message from Alcatraz:

ITS CRETZER. HE HAS THE GUN GALLERY OFFICERS
FORTYFIVE AND IS LIBERATING THE PRISONERS IN D
BLOCK. RIOT CALL SOUNDED. MOBILIZING ALL OFFI-
CERS. STAND BY.

I realized the riot would be a big one and it would be well led. Joseph Cretzer was a bank robber who had escaped from the McNeil Island Penitentiary by capturing a dump truck and crashing through the gates. After his recapture, Cretzer was found responsible for the death of a federal marshal whom he had assaulted after the escape. Cretzer had escaped from five other prisons. The next teletype read:

COY ALSO LOOSE WITH RIFLE AND TRYING TO PICK OFF TOWER OFFICERS. HAS WOUNDED TOWER OFFICER. DEPUTY MILLER ALSO WOUNDED. SITUATION STILL CRITICAL.

Bernard Coy was a degenerate bank robber who had sworn to us that he would never serve out his twenty-five-year sentence. He had also escaped from several prisons. Next, we learned over the telephone that a kidnapper was involved in the riot, an eight-time escapee who was serving a ninety-nine-year sentence. More phone calls told us that the ringleaders had been joined by a murderer, a psychopathic auto thief, a mentally retarded bank robber, a thief who had once fought an epic gun battle with FBI agents, and a small-time racketeer. Another teletype:

EIGHT OF OUR OFFICERS AMBUSHED AND LOCKED IN CELLS INCLUDING MILLER WHO HAS THE KEY TO REAR CELLHOUSE DOOR.

If the rioters searched these officers and discovered the key, they would let out scores of desperate men to roam all over the Rock. I teletyped back:

ORDER ALL WIVES AND CHILDREN TO LOCK THEM-SELVES IN THEIR APARTMENTS. EVACUATE MRS. JOHNSTON AND THE DEPUTYS WIFE IF POSSIBLE. CONTACT COASTGUARD FOR HELP AND FOLLOW RIOT PLAN STRICTLY.

We had anticipated possibilities of a major fire, hurricane, and riot, and we had prepared contingency plans on how each emergency was to be met. We had been particularly concerned that a prisoner might seize an officer's wife or child and talk his way out of prison on pain of putting the hostages to death. Now I feared that, amid the excitement, the riot plan might have been overlooked or forgotten. Twenty minutes passed until the next teletype:

THEY HAVE GONE MAD. CRETZER HAS SHOT THE CAPTURED OFFICERS. WE DONT KNOW HOW BADLY. WE ARE GOING IN AFTER THEM AS SOON AS WE GET THE OTHER PRISONERS CONCENTRATED IN THE WALLED YARD. THE MARINES ARE NOW HERE. EVERY ONE OF OUR OFFICERS HAS NOW REPORTED FOR DUTY. ASSOCIATE WARDEN MILLER NOW BACK AFTER WOUND HE RECEIVED WAS DRESSED.

The riot was becoming much more serious, but Cretzer and his men had not as yet found the all-important key. I directed my associates to get me aboard the first flight to San Francisco but found I could not reach Alcatraz for fourteen or fifteen hours. So I contacted the FBI headquarters, the Coast Guard, and the military authorities, as provided by the riot plan, and called for assistance. I telephoned the wardens at McNeil Island, Leavenworth, and Milan, Michigan, to detail cadres of selected officers to report to Warden Johnston at Alcatraz as soon as they could get there. The newspapers, radio, and TV people were pressing me for authority to go to Alcatraz. When I refused, they appealed to Attorney General Tom C. Clark, who upheld my decision. He suggested that I brief the newsmen as fully as I was able, and take them later to the island for eyewitness stories and pictures.

At 10 P.M. the teletype from Alcatraz said:

OFFICER STITES KILLED IN ATTEMPT TO STORM
GUN GALLERY. OFFICERS MAXWELL AND COCHRANE
AND OLDHAM WOUNDED BUT OFFICERS BERGEN AND
MAHAN NOW IN GUN GALLERY.

At 2:30 A.M., the word was more hopeful:

ALL HOSTAGES NOW RELEASED. PRISONERS WITH
GUNS HAVE BEEN DRIVEN TO COVER. DOOR TO D
BLOCK CLOSED. INMATES IN MAIN CELLBLOCK LOCKED
IN.

All night similar reports poured into Washington. Just as I boarded an airplane, I learned that Cretzer and Coy barricaded themselves in a utilities corridor and were shooting it out with our officers. Before dawn, no fewer than two hundred marine reinforcements landed on The Rock to help guard the other prisoners, and the Navy and Coast Guard sent small boats to patrol the Bay to pick up any swimmers. Then our men began to fire gas shells, and some badly aimed rounds set fire to patches of grass. Rumors were racing around San Francisco that the prison buildings were on fire as I began my flight to California.

Not until early morning did our officers succeed in breaking into the utilities corridor. One squad climbed on the roof, battered a hole, and dropped down hand grenades. Tank ammunition brought over from the arsenal at Benicia was fired down the corridor at point-blank range. There was a long silence— but when an officer looked out from behind cover, a shot rang out and a bullet hissed past his head. A storm of fire was now directed along the corridor and it seemed that no one could possibly survive.

When I arrived at San Francisco, a prison captain told me that all the rioters had surrendered except Cretzer and Coy, who had crawled into a narrow pipe tunnel and were still shooting it out. I hastily briefed the newsmen and headed for Alcatraz. When I reached the island an hour or so later, it was over.

Cretzer and Coy were laid out dead in the main corridor await-ing the inspection of the coroner.

Not until I had toured the close-custody cellblock D, strewn with spent cartridge casings and reeking with tear gas fumes, did I understand how it had been possible for the men to kidnap the officer in the gun gallery. We found some plumbing valves and fixtures ingeniously contrived and fitted together to form a jack screw. With this jackscrew and some pincers, they had managed to spread the bars of the gun gallery just wide enough for a man to wriggle and monkey-climb through. When the gun gallery officer's attention was diverted to the opposite end of the cellblock, a prisoner made it through the opening, slugged the guard as he came through the door and threw his gun down to the killers below.

I could now piece together the whole terrible and tragic affair. Our most carefully prepared armor had been broken. Two officers were killed and nine seriously wounded. Three convicts were in the morgue. The other prisoners were later tried, convicted, and executed. Five more were given additional sentences. The shooting was over and gradually the institution returned to normal, but its reputation as an impregnable prison had been fractured.

I was left in 1946 with no alternative but to retain Alcatraz as our maximum-security institution. I could not transfer men such as these to mingle with the mainland prisoners. The Cretzers and Coys had to be walled off. There were others equally dangerous and disruptive for whom we had no suitable institution. In the congressional hearings on the Department of Justice appropriations, where I suggested that a new maximum-custody prison must be built, I testified, "Alcatraz serves a very worthwhile purpose in taking out of the other federal institu-tions the prisoners who, if they were permitted to remain, would make necessary a much more repressive program and com-plicate rehabilitative opportunities. The really bad apples must be taken out of the barrel."

But during the years that followed, while we were opening

prisons without bars all over the country, Alcatraz seemed increasingly anachronistic. The G-men era was over; the Rock seemed also to be part of the past. The air of a tomb, a place of no return, was settling on the island, and even the fact that no man had ever escaped from Alcatraz was adding to my uneasy sense that I was presiding over an American Siberia. More serious to me was the fact that Alcatraz was now a symbol of retributive justice—the sort of tough prison that all prisons ought to be, according to many.

During the 1960's, financial considerations determined the issue and freed me from my dilemma. Alcatraz's buildings and steel towers were gradually being eroded by the salt spray, and would cost several million dollars to restore. The cost of supplying the island prison was exorbitant since food and water had to be brought across the bay. Alcatraz was also expensive to run, because it was located far from the continental center of population, far from most of the other prisons, and men had to be transported long distances from and back to the East and Middle West. The daily per-prisoner operating costs at Alcatraz were far higher than at any other federal institution. So we drew up plans for a new maximum-security prison to be built in the heart of the continent at Marion, Illinois, which could be built and operated at a lower cost. When the federal funds were made available for the new prison, we could close Alcatraz down.

In 1963, Attorney General Robert F. Kennedy approved its abandonment even though there were many congressmen, including the powerful chairman of the House Committee on Appropriations, Clarence Cannon, who believed that Devil's Islands of this type were the only answer to the escalating crime problem. There will always be the need for specialized facilities for the desperados, the irredeemable, and the ruthless, but Alcatraz and all that it had come to mean now belong, we may hope, to history.

THE GREAT ESCAPES

Ever since I joined the prison service, I have kept a logbook of great escapes. I have always understood why men facing long sentences would attempt wild stabs for freedom, even though the odds were formidably against them. It was part of my job to set up those odds, of course, because desperate men in mid-escape are more dangerous to the public than any other kind of criminal. It was also my lot to point out that escape is a futile way for anyone to solve serious problems. But I am an escape buff—fascinated by the Tower of London, the Castle of Chillon, and the circular cellhouses at the Illinois state prison at Joliet, not to mention Alcatraz. I admire the men who find ways to outwit their keepers, with their colorful plots and their meticulous ingenuity.

Only a dozen men out of the 750,000 held in the federal

prisons during my term in office were able to manage permanent escapes. Many hundreds more tried and failed. Very live men went out of prisons in undertakers' baskets, freight shipments, and garbage disposal consignments. They tried to fly over the walls, tunnel beneath them, climb over by day and night. Many men walked away from work details and out of the prison gates. The cleverest forged their release papers and left with the best wishes of the authorities. But they were almost always caught and brought back.

One of the first great escapes of my tenure occurred at Leavenworth. Francis L. Keating and Thomas Holden were serving twenty-five years for armed train robbery and figured they had little to lose by attempting a break. They worked on their sources in the prison office and persuaded an inmate clerk to issue printed passes entitling them to leave prison without escort for their work assignments. The passes were accompanied by photographs of the men, and were authenticated by the forged signatures of the associate warden. One day, Keating and Holden walked to the main gate, showed their passes, and strolled to a waiting car. Two years later, they were recaptured. Living in Kansas City, not fifty miles from the penitentiary, they had taken up golf, and some unsportsmanlike caddies recognized them and called the FBI. Before making the rearrest, the FBI agents chivalrously permitted Keating and Holden to finish their eighteen holes.

Another day, seven men forced their way out of Leavenworth at gunpoint. Led by Will Green, George Curtis, and Grover Durrill, they arranged to have guns smuggled into the prison in a barrel of shoe paste, and they also managed to get hold of some dynamite. Thus armed, they stormed into Warden Thomas White's office and seized him as a hostage, along with a secretary and two typewriter repair men. They rushed to the gate and threatened to blow up the hostages if it was not opened. Then they commandeered a passing car, released the secretary and repair men and drove off with the warden. Not far down the road, they shot him and tossed him into a roadside ditch, seriously wounded.

The prison officers and the police were angered by this cruel and senseless act, and took off in pursuit. They caught three of the men, and laid siege to a farmhouse in which the ringleaders were hiding out. Our men shattered the farmhouse with hand grenades and bullets and, behind a gas cloud, charged head on. Inside the farmhouse, three shots rang out—Green, Curtis, and Durrill killed themselves rather than give up, and their companion ran out the back door and turned himself in.

The most stylish escape of my prison career was that of Luis de Shelley, a counterfeiter, from the federal penitentiary at Atlanta. He was a member of the prison dramatic society and he planned a daring impersonation. One evening, while playing a female role, he walked off stage in women's clothes and up to the galleries, where he mingled with some citizens of Atlanta who had been invited to attend. When he found a woman whose baby was crying pitifully, de Shelley whispered to her that he was not particularly interested in the play and he offered to take the baby outside for a breath of fresh air. The mother gratefully handed her child to the thoughtful woman in the Mother Hubbard.

De Shelley walked down the stairs to the main corridor, pinching the baby so that it cried lustily. He ran to the main gate, wailing hysterically that the child was sick and had to be taken to a doctor. The gates were opened and de Shelley ran out, deposited the baby on the sidewalk, doffed his female garb, and escaped. He was not heard from for several years until federal agents traced some counterfeit notes that were unquestionably his handiwork. They made the re-arrest and brought de Shelley back to serve the rest of his sentence in the maximum-security prison at Alcatraz.

The traditional escape route from the penitentiary is the tunnel beneath the wall. Repeatedly we discovered tunnels burrowed alongside storm water drains that ran out beneath the walls, and we learned how to block the drains and flood the tunnels. In 1954, however, in one of those occurrences that teach prison officers humility and the danger of taking anything for granted, a man escaped from Atlanta through a water pipe just eighteen inches in diameter. It was the first time in seventeen years that anyone had broken out from behind the walls of Atlanta. He was George Ellis, and, from an account he sent me several years later, this is how he did it.

One day Ellis happened to notice a streak of green grass running through the ball field, leading to a grated manhole behind the handball courts. It was the source of a terracotta pipe line just eighteen inches across. "A tight fit for broad shoulders," he wrote me. "What scared me most was the thought of being trapped in there. What a way to die. But I wanted out of the penitentiary and started to make my preparations."

His tools were a pipe wrench, hammer, and chisel. He obtained an icebag for use as a water canteen and wrapped some civilian clothes in a plastic bag. He planned to hang a flashlight on a shoestring tied around his neck and to carry his watch, cigarettes, and matches in his cap. He would wear only shorts, a T-shirt, and tennis shoes.

Ellis picked a day for the escape when he could be absent from his work around the cellhouse without arousing suspicion. After telling a friend he planned to spend the day playing handball and sunbathing around the handball courts, he headed for the manhole grating. It was about 9 A.M. "Who would win the day, I thought to myself," Ellis wrote. "There was nothing casual in my thoughts as I looked up at the walls and tried to weigh the alertness of the gun tower guards. Could I worm along the tiny pipe, 250 yards or more, to the other side of the walls? Where would it lead to on the outside? It wouldn't take me long to find out."

Ellis sat near the manhole, and put on his tennis shoes. He was shielded from the nearest gun tower by a peach tree, and he was protected from fire from other gun towers by an earth

The pioneer English prison reformer
John Howard

WILLIAM MILLER, LONDON

HISTORICAL COLLECTIONS OF THE STATE OF NEW YORK

OPPOSITE TOP
Once such indignities as the pillory were society's answer to the crime problem

OPPOSITE BOTTOM
Prisoners at the State Prison, Auburn, New York, in the nineteenth century

Warden Gilbert Palmer (third from left) and his entire staff at the territorial prison, McNeil Island, Washington, c. 1890

The author as a cadet aviator,
Taylor Field, Montgomery, Alabama, November 1918

OPPOSITE TOP
Prisoner recreation area at Alcatraz

OPPOSITE BOTTOM
A view of the main cellhouse and staff housing area during the height of the 1946 riot.

A depiction of the 1946 riot

AU OF PRISONS

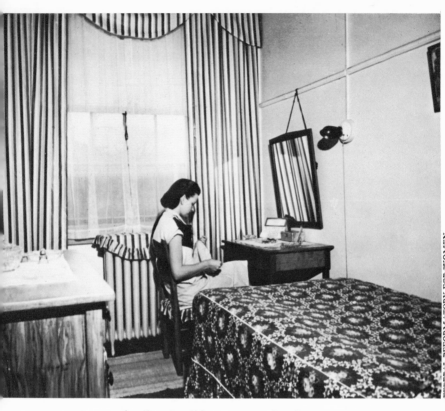

A cell at the Alderson women's prison

Sanford Bates,
director of the Bureau of Prisons,
1930–7, in 1963

The unfinished dome at Leavenworth

The author (left) escorting
Attorney General Robert F. Kennedy
on a tour of a federal prison

The control tower at the Marion, Illinois, maximum-security prison

A cell at Marion

The front gate of the Seagoville, Texas, prison

*View of the Robert F. Kennedy Youth Center,
Morgantown, West Virginia*

The author in 1969

tamper used for rolling the handball courts. He slid off the man-hole cover, wriggled into the pipe, and reset the grating. "This was no place for claustrophobic convicts. It took a bit of doing, but I crawled down the pipe head first, belly down, hunching along on my forearms. The first section of the pipe was dry. Hardly a blessing. Gravel and sand pebbles tore the skin off my arms and legs as I dragged myself along."

Ellis soon reached a junction of several pipes that emptied into a subterranean well. These other pipes were active, flowing sewage from the prison latrines into a main line that gradually enlarged. "It took an act of will for me to go on. Down the pipe and down a ladder into one of the subterranean wells I went. After a while, I was coated with slime, which at least made travelling easier as I slipped along." Then he reached the place where the sewage disposal system ran under the prison wall. It was blocked off by iron bars, and Ellis worked for two hours with his elementary tools to grind his way through. The bars had worn thin due to the constant erosion, but the air was un-believably foul. As he wrote me:

"Ironically, I thought of the adage, 'Water makes its own level.' Well, if this be my level, so be it. I never laid claim to being a knight in shining armor. The world is a mad, crazy place. One role is almost as good as the next. Maybe some day my role in life would change, but this was the day I was busting out of an escape-proof prison."

Overcoming his exhaustion, Ellis finished his work on the bars and squeezed through a hole. He crawled on for thirty more yards into a large, vaultlike chamber. This was akin to a shaft, reaching up to ground level, and above him Ellis saw a network of case-hardened steel bars put there to make escape impossible. "There was nothing to do now but rest, think and smoke. It looked like I had maneuvered myself to the point of no return. To go forward was impossible and to reverse only a little less so. How do you slide back up a greasy chute against a flow of four inches of filth?"

Ellis began to crawl back up the pipe and, reaching the gap in the bars, his body jammed against the jagged ends of metal. For the first time, he panicked, and in a frenzy he tore himself free. Then he could not get traction. He could not move except by feverish thrusts that barely inched him along. "There was no question of rest, as to stop was to become a clam soon submerged." His hope flickered and muscular spasms began. He knew only a brutish instinct for survival. When his arms gave out, he rolled on to his back and levered himself with his heels, and soon, when he felt the hard gravel tearing away the skin from his back, he knew he had made it to the first, hard section of the pipe. "I must have fainted a few times during the final stretch, but I pushed and pushed and finally saw the light of day. I was back where I had started."

After lying exhausted beneath the manhole grating for the rest of the afternoon, he took stock. He could make his way back into his quarters before the evening count. So Ellis painfully hoisted himself out of the pipe, closed the grating, walked undetected to the showers and scrubbed off the filth and dried blood. Changing into clean clothes, he was in time for the evening meal.

The rest of the week he spent preparing for a second attempt. "So fierce had the challenge now become that nothing short of a presidential pardon would dissuade me." Over and over in his mind he pondered the problem of the case-hardened steel network, and he decided to obtain a complex tool known as a "bar-spreader." To get this, he had to make a deal, and take another man out of Atlanta with him. "I will never reveal how I got the bar-spreader, but I soon had one that would break the walls of Fort Knox.

"The morning of the second attempt went perfectly. It was like riding the subway to suburbia. My arms were still sore from the first time, but I slit open a pair of socks and wore them on my forearms for protection. The dry pipe. The sprung bars. No problem. Then we used the bar-spreader on the case-hardened steel bars in the vault. It took us about half an hour to screw the pressure up and then the bar snapped like an icicle. We stepped through the gap, replaced the bar, passed through the vault and entered another pipe about three feet in diameter. We made out a faint light ahead of us. With the cagey caution of our kind, I moved forward alone to make sure that nobody had set a trap for me. But there was no need for alarm. The pipe ran out into a creek and, at 1.20 P.M., just as the prison's afternoon work whistle blew, my friend and I were free men."

George Ellis's escape was a classic—but we recaptured him three days later by means that I am still not able to reveal. He then committed his redoubtable energies to his own rehabilitation and became a model prisoner. He was paroled and released, and is now a respected citizen in a small town in the Middle West. Only a few of his friends know about his escape from Atlanta.

Two prisoners tried to get out of Leavenworth by simple and spectacular tactics. One man, while on a work detail near the towering wall, noticed that the wind there sometimes blew in great gusts. He found some canvas, made a parachute, climbed a water tower beside the wall and, when the next gust came, he tried to fly out of Leavenworth. He was swept off the tower and the parachute was sturdy enough to carry him to the ground, but inside the wall. He suffered a broken leg and the taunts of his fellow prisoners, and did not try again. The second man smuggled himself out in a crate nailed shut by two of his accomplices. Unfortunately, the freight handlers at Leavenworth station loaded the crate wrong side up and the prisoner, sick and fainting, was forced to call for help. Within an hour of his escape he was back inside the penitentiary.

A book, a play, and a motion picture named *The Desperate Hours* were made about the participants in another great escape. About six A.M. one day in 1952, fog began to roll in from the west toward the Lewisburg penitentiary. Half an hour later the officers in the gun towers reported the visibility was down to fifteen feet. At seven A.M. the officers in charge of the dormitories shouted that three men were missing. They were Joseph Wayne Nolen and Ballard French Nolen, two brothers serving twenty-five years for armed bank robbery along with a third brother, who had not joined the escape. Elmer Schuer, serving thirteen years for bank robbery, had accompanied the Nolen brothers in their venture. Together, they had fabricated a pipe ladder and slipped out of Lewisburg in the fog.

During the next eleven days, the two Nolen brothers and Schuer terrorized a family they held captive for nineteen hours —the desperate hours—and then they raided a gun store, robbed a bank, and headed for New York City. The police caught them in an uptown Manhattan apartment where they were drinking with three women, and a gun battle began. Both of the Nolens were killed, and so was a New York City detective. Only Schuer, hidden under a bed, survived, and he is now serving a ninety-five-year-to-life sentence in the New York state institution at Dannemora.

The part that appealed to me most in *The Desperate Hours* was the lesser-known role played by the third Nolen brother, John. After the escape was over and his brothers had been buried, he settled down resignedly to serve out his long term. He became an acolyte to the Catholic chaplain and was one of our best prisoners. He was paroled and, with hard work, astuteness, and dedication, won his way to the top ranks of the United Automobile Workers in Detroit.

At one point in his union career, Nolen ran into trouble and he asked me for help. The labor statutes forbade the election of former convicts to union office unless given what amounts to a certificate of good conduct by the parole board, and Nolen's election to a minor office was about to be set aside. So I appeared before the parole board and the Labor Department on Nolen's behalf and I was able to see to it that he was exempted from the disabilities of the act. Nolen has since distinguished himself in the UAW, and he is making a name as a determined contract bargainer.

On one occasion, I did not attempt to hide my sympathy for a prisoner who escaped from a federal reservation, but I could do nothing for him. Joseph Red Feather, a Sioux Indian, was timid, reserved, and a poor mixer, an easy target for the other prisoners at the Sandstone, Minnesota, correctional institution where he was serving a year and a day. One day Red Feather walked out of the institution—it was minimum-security—and he was brought back a few hours later and hauled up for disciplinary action. What bothered me about Red Feather, however, was not the escape but the sentence. The official records showed that a federal judge had given him his year and a day for this offense: "Having possession of a valid permit to sell one gray mare, he altered same to permit the sale of two mares." Sending a free-wheeling Indian horse trader to prison for a year for such an offense hardly seemed justice to me, so I did not punish Red Feather for his escape. He had been punished enough.

One of the very few men who did get away was Joseph Hogan, sentenced in 1926 to three years' imprisonment for auto theft. He was sent to Atlanta and, after working out well there, was transferred to a road camp in West Virginia. On June 14, 1927, he ran away, and he managed somehow to stay out of sight for thirty-one years. In December 1958 the FBI made the re-arrest in New York City, and the problem landed on my desk.

Hogan, it now turned out, was a model citizen, living in New York City under his own name, a widower bringing up five school-age children. He was an experienced roofer, although he was unemployed when the FBI caught up with him. Hogan also had an excellent war record. Again under his own name, he had joined the Army in 1942 and served until the end of the war, fighting as a tank driver from Normandy to the Rhine, winning the Silver Star for rescuing a wounded officer under fire. All things considered, it did not seem right for me to require that Hogan be returned to prison to serve out the rest of his term for auto theft, especially as he would under today's laws probably have been placed on probation as a first offender.

I took to the statute books and found my solution. The law that imposed additional punishment for escapes had not been enacted until 1930, and it seemed that Hogan might not legally be prosecuted for his escape in 1927. I also recalled that President Truman had issued an executive order providing that a criminal who enlisted in the armed forces between 1942 and 1945 could apply for executive clemency. So I consulted with William P. Rogers, attorney general in the second Eisenhower administration (later to be secretary of state in the Nixon administration), who agreed that executive clemency would be available. The prosecution decided not to contest the point and, almost thirty-two years after his escape, Hogan was released on his own recognizance and sent home to his family.

The one great escape I am waiting for will perhaps be made by a prisoner at Atlanta, one of whose names is Austin Wynn. He is a man in his late thirties who has spent more than twenty years in various prisons, escaping from two of them. He is a connoisseur's confidence man, whose principal enjoyment in life is the humiliation of law enforcement agencies.

Wynn's escape technique is the confidence trick of proportions so large as to be unsuspected. After serving a federal sentence for transporting forged securities across state lines, Wynn was sentenced to an additional term in a state institution, also on forgery charges. But he got a job as a clerk in the state prison record office, presiding over the flow of court orders, investigative reports, caseworkers' studies, and prison officers' correspondence with state officials. Wynn was a hard worker and he won the trust of his civilian supervisor. One day, a letter arrived at the prison from a state judge directing Wynn's release. Even though the signature was authentic, the letter would have been doublechecked had it not been accompanied by a transmitting memorandum signed by the attorney general of the state. This signature also appeared to be authentic. The final touch was a letter from Washington, from none other than the attorney general of the United States, withdrawing a federal warrant still outstanding against Wynn. This letter bore the distinctly illegible signature of Robert F. Kennedy.

The state prison authorities congratulated Wynn upon this turn in his fortunes, issued him a new suit, and paid the usual prisoner release gratuity of $1.50. The warden shook Wynn's hand and watched him go out the main gate. It was almost a month before the warden found that Wynn had forged all the documents, inserted them into old official envelopes, and included them with incoming mail. Then the warden learned that Wynn had stolen some of the prison's printed checks and was cashing them freely all over the state. He was posing as a promising young member of the state attorney general's office.

After a few more months, Wynn decided to go after federal game, and, on a visit to New Orleans, he printed up some vouchers drawable against the accounts of the Department of Justice. He also forged a set of FBI agent's identification cards and, cashing our checks, he traveled royally through the southern states. Then he went to South America, with a forged passport and travel documents, and made a good impression down there as a courteous tourist with a plentiful supply of travelers checks. He could probably have settled there for life.

In about a month's time, Wynn returned to the United States and journeyed about southern California in the guise of "Dr. Bartle Gilbert Wilson," the chaplain of the maximum-security prison at Alcatraz. He supported himself with paychecks made out to the Alcatraz chaplain and he was always able to tell civilians tales about prison life. But Wynn stayed in California too long. One morning as he presented himself in priestly attire to the desk clerk at a San Diego hotel, and asked to cash a check, the FBI arrived. In his belongings there were fifty-seven checks to be drawn against a federal reserve bank for sums totaling $132,800 and 850 checks to be drawn against the Justice Department for more than $1,000,000.

After Wynn served his sentence in the state prison he was transferred to us to work out his federal warrant. He wrote me a personal letter asking for help, but I sent him to the penitentiary at Atlanta. There he wrote poison-pen notes to the chaplain about his fellow prisoners and letters to governmental investigative agencies about alleged corruption. He even persuaded the FBI to look into charges of brutality by the guards and he threatened to sue the warden for violation of civil rights. Shortly before my retirement, I received a staff report on Wynn that concluded, "He is playing every angle—even working." I anticipate that his escape, if and when it ever comes, will be as brilliant in its way as George Ellis's tunnel saga.

Almost alone among Wynn's jailers, I held out hope and believed he might be rehabilitated. He has ambition and ability and it is not too late. Everything in life has been against him. His father abandoned the family. His mother was an epileptic who died in a state hospital when he was six. He was raised by his grandmother, a semi-literate who lived in a shack on an island in a river in the South, and who thought that the rest of the world had to be kept out. From the age of thirteen Wynn was a lawbreaker.

Not long ago, he wrote his grandmother a letter so full of lies about maltreatment at Atlanta that the warden who inspected the correspondence decided to write the facts to the elderly woman. The warden said the staff was treating Wynn as well as they were able, and, to his surprise, the woman replied. The warden sent the letter on to me. "Austin is a very nervous type," she wrote, "but warden, he is my grandson and he is my heart. I would to God I could take his place and he could go free, because he has a future before him, and I haven't. Of course, he did wrong, but most everyone of his age has made a mistake, one way or another. And he is more to be pitied than censured."

WOMEN BEHIND BARS

No one has really known what to do with the few women who are condemned to prison, least of all the federal government. The problem was first passed to the Honorable Herman Hoyt, acting U.S. attorney general, when cries of anguish were raised by Warden R. W. McClaughry of Leavenworth Penitentiary on July 3, 1906. One Lizzie Cardish, aged fifteen, had been unceremoniously left in his office by the U.S. marshal from the eastern district of Wisconsin. She had been given a life sentence for arson on an Indian reservation, a federal offense. The warden, not knowing what to do, and with no instruction from the faraway Department of Justice, gave this frightened and nervous child, as he described her, some lunch in the captain's office. Having no place for her at Leavenworth, he finally persuaded the warden of the nearby Kansas State Penitentiary to house her in the section set aside for women prisoners of the state until he could get word from the attorney general on how to handle his federal prisoner.

In any event, Lizzie Cardish remained in the state penitentiary until the following September, when the problem was neatly solved by commuting her sentence of life imprisonment. She was sent to a girls' training school and she stayed there until she was twenty-one. Then she was set free and sent home to the Indian reservation. Indians do not have much chance now when confronted with the Great White Father's Criminal Code but they had even less in Lizzie's day.

As time passed, other women convicted of federal offenses were remitted to federal penitentiaries, and the distracted officials farmed them out to state institutions whenever a place could be found for them. And conditions in some of these state prisons were so unspeakably bad that various women's groups began demanding that women be given decent conditions at least equal to those suffered by the men. They pointed to a report by the sociologist Frank Tannenbaum in the 1920's about a visit he had paid to a typical women's state prison in a southern jurisdiction. He wrote: "The dining room contains a sweatbox for women who are being punished by being locked up in a place with insufficient room to sit down and near enough to the table to smell the food. Over the table, there is a long iron bar, to which women are handcuffed when they are being whipped, and on the wall there is a sign—"Christ Died To Save Sinners."

A prisoner, Mrs. Kate O'Hare, once wrote of the women's wing of the Missouri state penitentiary at Jefferson City, "The first thing that struck me about the place was the dead, rancid odor, the concentrated smell of dead air, venerable hash, ancient stews and cabbage soup mingled with the rusty odor of decaying wood, grease and soap. Every crevice was inhabited by old and well-established cockroach families who insisted on sharing our meals. The rats were perhaps worst of all and, not until my young son visited me in prison and had the ingenuity to think of my covering the bars with wire, did I know a night's rest."

Federal women prisoners during the 1920's were lodged in these state prisons, county workhouses, city jails, and reformatories wherever the Justice Department could find room and board for them. But the Women's Christian Temperance Union, the General Federation of Women's Clubs, and other women's groups petitioned Congress for the construction of a modern federal prison in which women might at least be treated humanely. The first appropriation for housing units for federal women prisoners was passed by Congress in 1925. This was in response to a recommendation made by President Calvin Coolidge in his state of the union message—the only time, it is said, he suggested an expenditure of this type. Two years later the reformatory for women was opened at Alderson, West Virginia, a bleak West Virginia village. It was said that Alderson was an ideal spot because it was accessible to population centers and had good climate, water, and adjacent land for expansion. Actually, the location was dictated by the Republican National Committee. This posed a problem for Sanford Bates and the rest of us to try to develop a realistic rehabilitation program for women in this remote area.

The first fact about women's crime then and now is that there is very little of it—or at least only a few women are convicted. Today only one woman for every eight men is arrested in the country. Only one woman is imprisoned in federal, state, and local prisons for every twenty-five men. The reason for the difference between the arrest and imprisonment rate is that women are treated leniently. They do not commit the violent crimes most feared by the public and, as a result, they obtain mercy from grand juries, prosecuting attorneys, trial judges, and juries. Women also receive favorable treatment from prison officials, probation officers, and parole boards. All of this frequently led me to wonder why the public paid so much attention to such a relatively insignificant sector of the national fight against crime.

There is, on the other hand, much confusion of definition about women's crimes. There are probably more than one million abortions performed in the country every year. Department stores and supermarkets report a massive amount of shoplifting and petty larceny. Thousands of prostitutes and call girls operate in almost all of our cities. To what extent are these people to be regarded as criminals, if at all? But women also commit a sizable proportion of embezzlements that are never reported, and they blackmail men, and one another, with impunity. Women are often responsible for the crimes for which men are arrested and convicted, and they urge men to violence or accept stolen goods without complaint. Our confusion about women's crimes explains perhaps why we tend to view women criminals as pitiful and pathetic rather than villainous. Most women prison administrators still reflect the beliefs of Sarah Smith and Rhoda M. Coffin, the pioneers of the nineteenth-century women's prison reform, who wrote, "We must work for regeneration, the cleansing of the evil mind, the quickening of the dead heart, the building up of fine ideals. In short, we must bring the poor, sin-stained souls to feel the touch of the Divine Hand."

Women generally make better prisoners than men—and women's prison officials respond. Once the initial shock of imprisonment has passed, they are pleased that the matrons seem interested in their personal problems. They are grateful to the parole officers who find new friends and new jobs for them even before they are released. Prison officials of reformist bent therefore find work in women's institutions to be particularly rewarding. There is support from the prisoners, from most of the prison personnel, from the police, from the prosecutors, and from the public.

Women's prison officials find, on the other hand, that they have to be more watchful than at men's prisons to protect inmates from casual abuse. Not long ago in several state prisons women were whipped with leather straps for infractions of the rules. The American Correctional Association, in its manual for prison officers in charge of women, says, "One of the worst effects of corporal punishment is the loss of self-respect and the feeling of degradation that it engenders. Some institutions that do not practice it have devised punishments that produce the same effects: shaving prisoners' heads, dressing them in striped clothing, locking them in veritable dungeons and exposing them to the ridicule of other women. These and other forms of humiliating punishment should also be abolished.

Even though my jurisdiction was the federal system, in which there is no whipping, I was able to pass along information that helped put an end to abuse of women prisoners in the states. One male superintendent of a women's prison in North Carolina used to hold mock court in the middle of the night, white women on one side of the room and Negroes on the other, and he would issue and execute sentences of whipping on the spot—"anyone he happened to fancy that night," according to a welfare worker who helped us terminate this man's career. When a young Bennington College graduate complained recently that her physical examination upon admission to the New York City Women's House of Detention was cruel and callous, there was a public uproar. This led to several investigations of the prison and, eventually, to the decision to replace it.

Federal prison officials have been compiling information about the treatment of women prisoners in Arkansas, Mississippi, Louisiana, and Tennessee. One of our unofficial observers, on a recent tour of the Mississippi state prison farm at Parchman, asked a male guard about a leather strap hanging from a peg behind his office door in the women's wing. "Do you use that on the women, too?" The guard was in a genial mood, and, after making some comment about "mean niggers," he called a woman prisoner over and repeated the question. She said that sure the women were whipped and "Cap'n Joe can lift you right off the ground." He called over another woman, named "Treetops" because of her height, and "Treetops" thought the system worked fine.

In Mississippi, as in Arkansas, corporal punishment is specifically authorized by the state legislatures, and reform-minded governors make little headway with on-again, off-again prohibitions of the medieval practice. During the recent investigations of the Arkansas prison farms, it was also revealed that women prisoners were confined to their quarters day and night. Some said they were not allowed to speak for a period of eight months except to ask matrons questions.

My own administration of women prisoners in the federal system might best be characterized by the fact that they are not called prisoners or inmates, but "residents." I helped create women's open institutions and provided work, education, and vocational courses. I experimented with prison self-government and let selected women work outside the reformatories and return to their quarters at night. The states of New Jersey, California, and Wisconsin also moved ahead in women's prison reform and were soon scarcely treating women as criminals at all. New Jersey's Brookfield Farm is preeminent in the nation, and its late warden, Edna Mahan, was the most widely quoted authority on women's imprisonment.

The Alderson reformatory has been fortunate in that it has had several pioneering, able, and imaginative women as wardens. Miss Mary B. Harris was the first superintendent—she would permit no one to call her warden—who set the pattern and course of the institution. It was to be as nearly as possible like and old-fashioned girls' school, guiding its pupils with compassion and understanding along the paths of righteousness. She was succeeded by Helen Hironimous, an equally considerate leader but more practical and aware of the facts of life. Miss Nina Kinsella, the third warden, received the Federal Women's Award for outstanding achievement for the able and innovative manner in which she administered the institution. The present warden, Miss Gladys V. Bowman, has carried forward these traditions. Under her leadership it has become one of the outstanding women's institutions of its kind in the world. Visitors come from every nation to see it; interns are trained here for service in state agencies; research in abnormal behavior of women is conducted there as well as experimentation in the kinds of vocational training most likely to promote the rehabilitation of women offenders.

Amid the sunny, scenic roll of the Blue Ridge foothills two separate clusters of two-story cottages have been built. These form an upper and lower campus of dormitories of colonial architecture. Over-all it reminds visitors of a girls' college or a research institute. There is an average population of 450 to 500 residents. They are a cross-section of federal law breakers. A considerable proportion are narcotics addicts, but there are also a generous number of young girls who steal cars, a few quite expert check forgers, and some high-powered bank embezzlers. As a matter of fact the largest bank defalcation ever discovered was committed by a woman who eventually was sent to Alderson. Not a few are thieves and a small number are "madams" who transport prostitutes across state lines. One in three of the Alderson residents is under twenty-five. Yet, surprisingly enough, few are there because of offenses involved with sex.

Alderson over the years has developed an impressive variety of training courses. A career staff of more than two hundred people—one to every three residents—conducts the basic elementary and secondary classes of an accredited public school in addition to custodial duties. There are courses in shorthand, typing, and filing acceptable to accredited business schools. The residents are trained as beauticians and work in small garment shops. They are paid for their prison chores. In one program, the residents operate IBM key punch machines, verifiers, varitypers, and elementary calculators. The state of West Virginia issues certificates of proficiency to residents who pass their business courses and makes no mention that the diplomas were earned in prison.

Discipline at Alderson is handled calmly, and very little is needed. Residents who are reported for infractions of the rules appear before an "adjustment committee," comprising a custodial, medical, and one other officer. The offense is discussed with the resident and, depending upon her attitude, the degree of the offense, and the staff's knowledge of her personality and background, action is taken accordingly. This is usually a warning or suspension of privileges. In serious cases administrative segregation is imposed.

Alderson has an adequate hospital, including a maternity ward in which an average of twenty babies are born to new residents every year. We always did our utmost to ensure that this moment was as pleasurable to the residents as circumstances permitted. The babies are tended in the hospital during the early weeks, and they are the most popular and frequently visited members of the population. Unfortunately, or so it seems to the residents, the babies may not stay, and they are sent to the father's or the mother's relatives or friends, as she chooses. The state of West Virginia issues birth certificates that bear no note of any kind that the babies were born in prison.

The women who are sent to Alderson reflect the times in which they live. The first resident, with the designation 1-W, served a one-year sentence for violating the Volstead (Prohibition) Act. Her fellow prisoners were for the most part elderly lady bootleggers and moonshiners from mountain communities not unlike those around Alderson. In recent years, they have tended to come from fragmented urban surroundings. One typical resident was a nineteen-year-old convicted of stealing a check and forging it, as instructed by her husband, to get money for drugs. Another was an illegitimate child who had left school at thirteen because she was pregnant—one of the possible fathers being her mother's lover—who had capped a young life of violence by stabbing another woman with a knife. Warden Bowman's records reveal many such sad stories.

One prisoner in serious trouble was Sally, fifteen years old when she was committed to Alderson to serve a five-year sentence under the federal juvenile delinquency act. Sally had run away from a poor home when she was eleven and married three times before she came to us, the second and third time bigamously. Three times she escaped from Alderson—once by cutting the screen out of her cottage window and sliding down knotted blankets, once by running away from a blackberry-picking excursion, once by joining a group of girls in an attack on several matrons. She was always caught and brought back. After many years of fruitful work in the reformatory Sally earned her parole, and she was sent back to her mother. But two months later, she ran away from home and left her mother a note, "It wouldn't work. You can't be happy living with my ways. I know what this means. I'm just no good." Sally was arrested as a parole violator and, back at Alderson, she sank into a slump. Her sense of inadequacy was so profound we could do little for her. She served out her sentence, was released, and disappeared.

Then there was Gypsy Ellen, who came to us with a sentence of seven years and three months, with an additional probationary period of five years to follow. Her offense was the ruining of a helpless widow in a confidence trick known in Gypsy parlance as a *bajour*. Gypsy Ellen, a palmist and fortune teller, persuaded the widow to cash ten thousand-dollar bonds, sell her property, and draw out almost every cent she had in the bank. Gypsy Ellen promised that with the help of a mysterious spirit she would duplicate the widow's shiny new hundred-dollar bills with similar ones for a small commission. While mumbling her incantations and seemingly going into a trance, Gypsy Ellen disappeared with the money. The gullible old woman collapsed into a paralytic state. She was able, however, to direct the police to the hiding place of Gypsy Ellen who, despite her claims of innocence, was convicted.

Lois was a pathological liar who was sent to Alderson for impersonating an employee of the federal government. She had also lived in the guise of "Paula Carol von Luckner," purportedly the niece of the famous German sea raider of World War I. She often talked about von Luckner as "Uncle Felix" and said,

"He told me long ago that he was sick of war and would never fight again." Lois, boasting plausibly about her uncle, posed as an attorney for the lands division of the Department of Justice. She, with the help of a man with whom she was living, fleeced a real estate dealer out of a near fortune.

Kay was a demure college graduate who used her art store as a front for an "escort" service and who tried to boost the desirability of Chicago as a convention town. She assembled a bevy of call girls but was too avaricious in her demands on some "fresh stock" she had brought to Chicago for a political convention. The girls rebelled and snitched to the FBI. At Alderson Kay spent her time in the arts and crafts department. She carried on an intense correspondence with her daughter, who helped her to change. Upon her release, she set up a new home, obtained honest work, and kept in touch with us. She wrote her caseworker at the reformatory, "It is true that at times one is discouraged, but after all we usually get what we ask for. If you play, you must pay. I think that when one has paid enough, destiny has a way of taking care of us."

Not even the notorious gun molls are beyond hope of rehabilitation. These women usually have their emotions under control and can perceive the advantage of educational and training opportunities not available to them in the deprived areas from which many came. We had custody for many years of Kathryn Kelly, the wife of Machine Gun Kelly. Kathryn was sent to Alderson with a life sentence for kidnapping and so was her mother, another member of the organization. She was alleged to be the brains of the Machine Gun Kelly gang.

In our diagnostic studies, we learned that Kathryn had been married four times between her fourteenth and twenty-sixth birthdays. During the late 1920's she ran a shady hotel with her mother in Fort Worth and she became associated with criminals. She was arrested twice for shoplifting. She was also sentenced to five years' imprisonment for robbery in Oklahoma, but the conviction was reversed upon appeal. In 1930, Kathryn married Machine Gun Kelly and that road led to Alderson.

In the reformatory, Kathryn and her mother were good prisoners. Kathryn developed an interest in gardening and became an accomplished worker in the greenhouse. Her mother was a seamstress in one of the garment shops. Neither gave up hope for their eventual release and they took advantage of the educational training programs—but the parole board would not let the survivors of the Kelly gang go. Machine Gun Kelly died in Leavenworth in 1954. Not long afterward, Kathryn and her mother were finally released upon a court reversal of their conviction. They had served twenty-five years.

At 2:30 A.M. on the day following Kathryn Kelly's release, the telephone rang in Warden Bowman's quarters at Alderson. The former gun moll was phoning long distance from Oklahoma. She had served more time in prison than most murderers, and she vowed to Warden Bowman: "I'll never be back." She never has been.

Women's prison life—and underlife—is wholly different from that of men's prisons. Women do not form the cohesive mass that exists inside men's prisons, and they build their own groups and organizations for their own reasons. There is less need for formal defenses because they often regard the matrons as substitute mothers. But there is great need for defenses against the pressures that constitute a more subtle attack on the mind. The federal prisons have been able to quench the physical abuse of women prisoners but, in the psychological field, we have much to learn.

What does the prison experience mean for them? The testimony of released women is quite clear. The sharpest edge is the deprivation of personal autonomy. For women more than men, the limiting of movement, the regulation of schedule, the restrictions of contact with families, the petty detail of organization life are irksome in the extreme. The residents of Alderson must fall in line for counts and the bells ring much as they do in men's penitentiaries. Residents must sign out for prison functions, field exercises, and sick call. They are much more resentful than men about their inability to change prison regulations they find ridiculous, such as the precisely detailed manner in which clothes must be laid out in the closets and bureaus.

Women prisoners particularly object to the loss of personal effects. On arrival in prison they must strip and most of their personal clothing and belongings are listed, packaged in brown wrapping paper and mailed off to family or friends. They bathe beneath the eye of prison officers and are examined carefully for infection. One of the sociology researchers who spent some time at Alderson ascribed some of the difficulty in motivating the women to participate in various programs to their clothing. She said:

"The attack upon the individual's self-image with reference to clothing is particularly acute. The effort of some of the women to individualize the prison issue by the simple hand-working of a monogram on a blouse, or strategic placement of pleats on a surplus WAC jacket in an attempt to make them seem more like 'free world' clothes, are all evidence of the subtlety of deprivation."

Women prisoners also resent the dominant position of other women prison officers, whom they often like as individuals, and they do not live well with the fact that all of their fellow prisoners are women. "The hardest part of living in prison is to live with another woman," said one resident. "To live with other women is to live in a jungle," said another. "I never tell another woman anything important."

The unavailability of heterosexual relationships leads to lesbianism, to a greater or lesser extent, in all women's prisons in the United States. Every effort is made to minimize it by isolating the "studs"—those who take the masculine role—and by punishing those apprehended in compromising situations. But it exists, just as homosexuality does in men's prisons, and no one has come up with an answer to the problem. The lesbian relationships are quite complex, in that women prisoners form their own "families" in which they feel secure. There are simple husband and wife relationships, with mistresses and rivals, and there are mother and daughter relationships, with aunts, cousins and nieces, in which the older women look after the younger. Within the families, loyalty is very strong and other prisoners are not of the same world. Everybody's enemy is the "jive bitch" who spreads lying stories in order to create discord in families, or who gossips with prison officers about family affairs.

Although there is some violence in women's prisons (usually bloodied noses in sudden rumbles), women tend to enforce their codes peacefully. One field observer noted verbatim a recent conversation in an Alderson dining room in which a resident was warned that she had offended against group mores.

BETH: Hey, what do you think of an inmate that thinks she's an officer? You know who I mean, don't you? You dig it? She likes to give another inmate orders like an officer. Say, don't she know that she's got five numbers across her chest like the rest of us?

JEAN: Maybe she forgot. Maybe she thinks that she's here for a vacation in the mountains. Yeah. Here for the season and not for a reason.

Laughter from all the other residents at the table.

BETH: You *sure* you know who I mean?

THE OTHERS: Yeah.

The false loyalties built up in a women's institution, the lesbianism, the stigma inherent in a prison sentence, and the dubious value of sending women to prison as a deterrent to similar acts raise the question of need for such an instrumentality in our culture. The imprisonment of women in a modern state is not only abnormal for those who suffer it but it may also be doing more harm than good except for a few who commit serious crimes of violence.

The rehabilitation of women prisoners is especially difficult because inspiring personnel to fill the routine operating posts

are hard to recruit. The matrons who seek employment in federal and state institutions for the most part do so because it offers
work that is relatively high paying in the rural areas where
most such institutions are located. The matrons are usually the
beneficiaries of civil service tenure, good pensions, and a degree
of self-satisfaction not found in the garment factory or check-
out counter. I have encountered few, if any, who seek such
employment because they are at heart malicious misanthropes,
as some novelists would have us believe. Those who are impatient, gruff, or domineering are shunted off to work requiring
little contact with the prisoners. There is in fact a particular
hazard of work in a women's institution—the threat of charges
of lesbianism. The inmate who makes this charge usually has
little to lose, and matrons find they must conduct themselves
with extreme care to avoid suspicion.

If all prisons as now conceived and operated have a doubtful
future, then women's prisons will disappear first, in my opinion.
Already, the confinement of women has virtually been abandoned in many states. In New England there were only 353
women in prison in the fall of 1967—ranging from 1 in New
Hampshire, 8 in Vermont, and 18 in Rhode Island to 129 in
Connecticut and 144 in Massachusetts—and a similar situation
exists in the North Central states. How can the costs of a correctional apparatus for these handfuls be justified to the taxpayers? One answer might be to form "regional prisons" for
women, although this might conflict with state laws and might
also be ruled unconstitutional. Also, if women may best be rehabilitated close to their families, why dump them into regional
pools? We must find substitutes—more probation, commitment
to a foster home, a mental institution, or directly to a work-
release halfway house.

Women are not likely to be deterred from their "typical"
crimes by the improbable threat of imprisonment. These crimes
are usually impulsive instances of shoplifting, check-forging,
drug-taking and illicit sex activity, as we have seen, for which

clinical observation and community treatment are suitable. The occasional major women criminals—embezzlers, blackmailers, and murder-for-hire planners should obviously receive the sternest sanction of the law. But where should these women be sent, and who should pay?

My own feeling is that we should stop kidding ourselves about the small and poorly equipped state women's prisons and start looking for new concepts. The public is ready in women's cases for a much greater use of probation, halfway houses, and community shelters and clinics. For those few women who must be incarcerated I believe the federal government must assume the responsibility—assuming that, whenever the criminal's residency is established, the cost would be charged back to that state or locality.

The federal prisons would receive the serious women criminals—and the rest of the women's prisons in the United States should be shut down.

THE VIPs

Andrew, if I should not see you again, I wish you to remember and treasure up some things I have already said to you: In this world, you will have to make your own way. To do that, you must have friends. You can make friends by being honest, and you can keep them by being steadfast. You must keep in mind that friends worth having will, in the long run, expect as much from you as they give you. To forget an obligation, or be ungrateful for a kindness, is a base crime. Men guilty of it sooner or later must suffer the penalty.

> *Advice to Andrew Jackson from his mother*

One of the reasons I admire President Harry S. Truman is that I know, from personal experience, that he is the embodiment of the steadfastness to friends so extolled by Jackson's mother.

To survive in Washington requires no more talent, diligence, and good sense than in other cities and lines of work, but loyalty to one's friends and associates and, in my case, prisoners, is a necessity. In our bureaucratic universe there are many SOBs, but they are "our SOBs" to be defended against the enemies of prison reform.

Truman was still a senator from Missouri when I first met him. He owed his nomination and election less to the greatness that he would later demonstrate as President than to the chicanery of Boss Tom Pendergast and the Kansas City Democratic machine. In 1937 Pendergast was indicted for fraud by a Kansas City grand jury and he was subsequently sentenced in federal court to a short term of imprisonment. The instigator of the proceedings was U.S. Attorney General Frank Murphy, who had succeeded Homer S. Cummings in the Roosevelt administration.

The morning of the day Pendergast was due to be committed to Leavenworth, I was telephoned by Duke Shoop, the Washington correspondent of the Kansas City *Star*, who said he wanted to print the prison "mug shot" of Pendergast complete with prison numbers. I was a good friend of Shoop's but I explained it was against our policy to expose prisoners to unwanted publicity or shame or to ridicule them. The days of the pillory had ended in the eighteenth century. Shoop said he understood, but he was going to get the picture. Fifteen minutes later, the "hot line" from the attorney general's office buzzed on my desk. Murphy wanted to know why I would not cooperate with the *Star* and, even though I explained our policy, he ordered me to release the picture of Pendergast. To make sure I complied, Murphy signed and sent the telegram to the warden of Leavenworth himself.

Pendergast's prison picture was printed in large dimensions on the front page of the *Star*. A prisoner tossed a copy into Pendergast's cell with a snide comment, whereupon Pendergast fell back on his bunk, clutching his chest and gasping for breath.

Fortunately an alert guard noticed his condition and summoned doctors just in time to save Pendergast from what might have been a fatal heart attack.

Truman telephoned me at once about this regrettable incident. "Bennett," he snapped, without preliminary courtesy, "you have Tom Pendergast in Leavenworth. I want you to know that he's a friend of mine. I'm not going to forget him even though he's in prison." Here was interference from the other side, and I merely replied, "Yes, sir." Then Truman began to speak much more pleasantly, and at the end of our talk, he said, "I'm not asking any favors for him, do you understand, but I want him treated no differently from anybody else." Truman meant that he did not expect Pendergast's privacy in prison to be violated again, or that Pendergast would be given a hard way to go. Later I saw Pendergast in Leavenworth, and when I inquired how he was getting along he said: "Don't worry about me. I'll make it and I'll lick those guys outside yet." Pendergast recovered, took part in prison work and recreational activities, and was released. He later expressed his gratitude to me for the fair treatment he had received, and so did Senator Truman.

When he became President, Truman, who never forgot a friend or a favor, showed he appreciated my attitude vis-à-vis Attorney General Murphy, and he threw his redoubtable energies into the prison reform movement. His most typical contribution was to secure the enactment of a pension improvement plan for the prison career staff, which did more for the morale of our service than most of our congressional successes.

Murphy, a compassionate man, an advocate of civil rights, and a defender of the FBI, was elevated to the Supreme Court by President Roosevelt and replaced by the dynamic Robert H. Jackson. It was Jackson's successor, our wartime Attorney General Francis Biddle, who summed up Murphy unforgettably. He wrote in his memoirs, "Murphy had no administrative competence. He was vain, self-conscious, and avid for publicity.

He was like a ham actor, beating his chest, stepping aside, throwing his head up, darting a piercing look. Murphy believed in his God, in his country, in himself, a trinity that fused and merged, spiraling ever upward." This in my judgment is too harsh a picture of Attorney General Murphy, but it is easy for me to understand how a man so different from Murphy as Francis Biddle could dislike his predecessor.

Biddle became one of my closest friends, and he, more than any of the cabinet officers I served, made frequent visits to the federal prisons. He was very interested in the prisoners, as he put it, "with their strange lingo, their touching struggle, their hopelessness," and he upheld most of my recommendations. At Atlanta, while attending one of my presentations of awards to model prisoners, he received a tribute from the prison newspaper as a man whose "humanitarianism is a conviction rather than a convenience." At Alcatraz, he insisted on lunching in the main dining room even though he had been warned that a prisoner had recently struck the warden on the back of the neck with a hard tray during just such a casual meal.

On a visit to Alderson, his wife Katherine, a minor poetess, read to the residents one of her poems about "blackshirt cruelty," "the goosestep mine," and "the salt in our blood and our bone shape." The Alderson *Eagle* commented that the residents had enjoyed Mrs. Biddle's recitation, "feeling the spirit of America swell and pound about their ears."

Biddle, an elegant man, was delighted that day at Alderson when one of the Negro residents gave birth to a baby boy and said her choice for names lay between Joe Louis and Francis Biddle. Instead, she chose Napoleon Bonaparte, but Biddle told her he was honored to have been considered.

Biddle was a connoisseur of correspondence. He sent me a memorandum he had received from FDR that he treasured, which had accompanied approval of commutation of sentence for moonshining. It read: "Send word to Claude W. Blackman that the President of the United States expects him to go straight, keep sober, to make no more whiskey and to take care of his family." I was not to be outdone, and I sent to Biddle, for transmission to FDR, a grateful letter I had received from one of my ex-prisoners: "I write to tell you how much your training has meant to me. When my new case just came up in Tennessee court, they all showed off my new still. The judge and jury all looked it over most carefully and admitted to a man that it was the finest piece of coppersmithing they had seen in these parts, barring none. I just wanted you to know I owe it to your sheet metal course in vocational training."

One of my favorite anecdotes concerns Herbert Brownell, the first attorney general in the Eisenhower administration, who sat beside me one day at Alderson while I was listening to some of the residents' grievances. A girl asked if I would give her permission to have a tattoo removed from her stomach. I looked at Brownell and we nodded our approval. Not long afterward, Brownell received a letter of thanks at his office, which was opened by his staff, that began: "Hey, remember me, the girl with the tattoo?"

During and after World War II, the federal prison system played host to several VIPs. I found that these men, facing what must have been a considerable ordeal, for the most part heeded the biblical injunction: "Whatsoever is brought upon thee, take cheerfully, and be not cast down when thou art changed to a low estate, for gold is tried in fire and acceptable men in the furnace of adversity."

One very important prisoner who became a friend was the legendary Governor James Curley of Massachusetts. At the age of seventy-two, he was convicted of mail fraud in connection with war and defense housing contracts and was sentenced to six to eighteen months' imprisonment. He had been three times mayor of Boston, twice a member of Congress, twice governor, and he considered himself far from his last hurrah. Curley's counsel pleaded in court that imprisonment would be tantamount to a death sentence because his client had a weak heart and had lost part of his stomach in surgery, and there he was, sitting in court in a wheelchair with bowed head and trembling hands. On arrival at the correctional institution at Danbury, Connecticut, however, Curley pushed the wheelchair aside. "I don't need that," he said. "They think I'm pretty sick but I'll show them."

Curley took an active interest in the rehabilitation programs at Danbury and got along excellently with the other prisoners. He was a fascinating talker, of course, and he loved to regale the men with tall tales about his political career. He always had an Irish joke for everybody, and his good humor was infectious.

One of his favorite diversions was to read out loud from Shakespeare. Soon we noticed that the prisoners were beginning to quote from Shakespeare in their letters. The janitor who cleaned the hallway outside Curley's quarters closed a letter to his wife: "There is some soul of goodness in things evil, would men observingly distil it out." A prisoner wrote to a federal judge requesting revision of his sentence despite "the fine quillets of the law." In the cell of one man who drove his mates to distraction with his protestations of innocence, a penciled note was delivered: "To thine own self be true and it must follow as the night the day, Thou canst not then be false to any man."

When Curley was released, he told us he felt ten years younger, and he looked it. He roared back to Boston and was given a triumphal reception at the railroad station.

In 1949, Congressman J. Parnell Thomas was sent to Danbury to serve a short sentence for making false claims and conspiracy against the United States, in other words, for padding his congressional payroll and taking kickbacks from his staff. The powerful chairman of the Un-American Activities Committee was a difficult prisoner, belligerent and stubborn, and he seethed with resentment when he was told he would get no special privileges. Thomas was disliked by his fellow prisoners and this contributed to a persecution complex. I was surprised when Thomas told his parole board he was learning from his prison experience and said, "My vacation from society has added years to my life." Several years after his release, however, Thomas published an article in *Life* that was truer to type, bitterly critical of Danbury and its staff, the parole board, and me. Thomas's problem was that he had few of the inner resources upon which men are able to fall back in adversity.

During this period, I was frequently called upon to provide "discipline, care and treatment" for federal prisoners who had been convicted of various offenses that reflected the disquiet about Communist infiltration. The most prominent of these was Alger Hiss, once a law clerk to Oliver Wendell Holmes, an assistant secretary of state under Edward R. Stettinius, who had been sentenced to five years' imprisonment for perjury following his confrontations with Whittaker Chambers. Hiss, prisoner No. 19137, was assigned to Lewisburg and as well as any man I had known he accepted his lowly lot. He was assigned to one of the storerooms as a clerk, was active in the choir and Bible discussion groups, and he spent most of his spare time reading and studying in the prison library. His fellow prisoners unquestionably liked him. Although the reports that reached me from Lewisburg about Hiss were good, the correspondence from the public was vitriolic. The consensus of my mail was that Hiss had been saved from treason charges only by the statute of limitations, and ought to be treated severely in prison.

The Hiss issue reached its height when, as a model prisoner, he was granted time off his sentence for good behavior. This reduced his time to be served in prison to three years, eight months. There was a public uproar of which I was the principal victim. Speaking into the wind, I explained that time off for good behavior was one of the crucial elements of prison reform and that all men must be given an incentive for rehabilitation. As far as I was concerned, Hiss was just another prisoner.

When Hiss was due for release in 1954, the letters took on a violent tone and I could not disregard the possibility that someone might try to kill him as he left Lewisburg. So we closed off the prison and the grounds, stationed armed guards around the entrance gate, and worked out a combined security plan with the Pennsylvania state police. Fortunately, Hiss was set free uneventfully and, after making a brief statement and posing for press photographs, he drove off with his wife and his attorneys.

In one of the most tragic incidents of my administration, William Remington, a former Commerce Department official convicted of perjury during these investigations of Communist infiltration, was murdered in a federal prison. While serving his three-year sentence in Lewisburg, Remington was persecuted by a prisoner named George McCoy who said that he wanted to "get me a Commie." One night McCoy and another prisoner named Louis Junior Cagle brained Remington with a brick. I was horrified. Such was the temper of the times that, following Remington's death, rumors were spread that he had been involved in a homosexual attack upon another prisoner, who had killed him in self-defense. These rumors persisted until McCoy and Cagle were tried for committing murder on a federal reservation and were sentenced to life imprisonment.

During the 1950's McCarthyism, growing out of the public concern about Communist infiltration, spread through Washington like a plague. The steadfastness of our friendships and our mutual loyalties were put to the test as rarely before. One nerve-wracking episode began for me, as it must have for many public servants, when a disgruntled ex-employee publicly charged me with softness on Communism and offered no evidence to support the preposterous accusation. He was a prison warden whom I had let go for nonperformance of duties. I was hailed before Senator Pat McCarran's Senate subcommittee on appropriations without any notice of the subject of the inquiry. I was not allowed to bring any of my associates, even though it was presumably an open session.

To my astonishment, Senator Homer Ferguson of Michigan began pugnaciously to read off quesions from sheets of typescript that had been supplied to him, as I learned later, from the ex-warden. He was accusatory and gruff in his cross-examination for reasons I could not understand, but because he was a United States senator with a voice in our funding I struggled to hold my temper lest our employees and the innocent inmates of our prisons would suffer. Ferguson's general point of attack was that I had made it easy for prisoners in Danbury to maintain Communist connections and that my whole bureau was soft on Communism. I answered the questions and was dismissed without being permitted to make a general statement, correct the record, file supplemental answers, or produce testimony of the records involved. This was a "star chamber" proceeding if ever there was one.

When no further formal hearings were scheduled, I knew that I must wait for vindication in the course of events. I was told I was considered by no one to be soft on Communism, and that Ferguson was merely attempting to make a political case against the Truman administration and its attorneys general, Tom C. Clark, J. Howard McGrath, and James P. McGranery.

This experience was an ordeal, however, and I was grateful for a measure of public support from many friends. One of these was Senator William Langer, a North Dakota Republican, a senior member of the Senate Judiciary Committee, who called me to his office one day and said he meant to set the record straight. "Wild Bill" Langer had long been interested in prison reform and had been grateful when we accepted for treatment in one of our mental hospitals a life-termer who could not be cared for in North Dakota. We had become better acquainted when Langer himself was convicted for the misuse of state and federal funds, was acquitted, and set free by a federal court of appeals. Now Langer rose on the Senate floor and made a passionate speech in my defense. Another friend, Senator Wayne Morse of Oregon walked over to Langer and calmed him, so that the oration would be more effective. Langer's intervention was particularly welcome because civil servants are not often able to enter the public forum to answer charges made against them. The advice of Andrew Jackson's mother about how one can make friends by being honest and keep them by being steadfast is one reason why I treasure Bill Langer's memory.

The presidential election of 1952 returned the Republicans to power for the first time in twenty years, and the question was whether President Eisenhower and the moderates around him would be able to keep McCarthyism in check. During the interregnum before Eisenhower took office, several FBI agents appeared at our reformatory at Petersburg, Virginia, without prior reference to me. The warden was told that the FBI men were there to look into charges of "irregularities," under an old executive order that empowered the FBI to "investigate irregularities in federal penal institutions."

In view of what had transpired before, I concluded that the FBI had now been brought into the "softness on Communism" campaign and I was sure the matter was now serious. They were making the investigation without the request or approval of the attorney general, because there was no attorney general, and they did not even bother to inform the acting attorney general.

The ten and sometimes twenty FBI special agents who swarmed over the Petersburg institution checking our books and records, questioning the personnel, interviewing the prisoners, and listening to the complaints of disgruntled former employees found nothing of any significance. They reported what they believed to be the disappearance of several hams, one or two alleged instances of homosexuality, and some unrecorded absences of personnel, all on the basis of anonymous information. The warden felt sure his phone was tapped, but he talked on and on to me, hoping, as he wrote me privately, that the FBI would get an earful.

The prisoners were aware of all this and some were delighted to see their guards under fire. Others resented the intrusion. The situation grew so delicate that the warden feared a riot or disturbance of some other kind. When matters got worse, I informed FBI Director Hoover that after a certain date I would no longer permit questioning of the prisoners without a written order from the attorney general or a specific statement of the exact irregularity being investigated. On that note the so-called investigation came to a halt.

When President Eisenhower was inaugurated and Herbert Brownell became attorney general, these FBI reports and the records of Senator Ferguson's interrogation were sent to Brownell's office. He looked into some of the reports himself and asked his deputy, William P. Rogers, to examine the rest. Now I was given ample opportunity to present my side of the story and I was heard, patiently, understandingly, and objectively. Brownell and Rogers were Republicans and I was a Democrat. They could easily have found grounds to recommend that I be replaced, and already several others were angling for my job. Rogers, however, informed himself in detail on the Bureau of Prisons and recommended that I be retained in office. President Roosevelt had set a precedent by reappointing Sanford Bates as director in 1933 even though Bates was a Republican. President Eisenhower would have the opportunity to discard the precedent and appoint a Republican if there was the slightest reason to believe that I was soft on Communism or ineffective.

President Eisenhower turned out to be, however, the fourth in line of Presidents who would support prison reform. He studied the recommendations of Brownell and Rogers that I be retained in office, and approved them. I was relieved, indeed, when I was reappointed to my position, and considered this a vindication of my integrity as a public servant.

I was even more relieved that Eisenhower, Brownell, and Rogers showed themselves determined to rid the country of McCarthyism as soon as possible, and it was a pleasure to work for them. Rogers's wife, Adele, incidentally, helped make it possible for me to bury the memories of the "Petersburg probe." The dinners and other social gatherings she and Mrs.

Brownell fostered brought J. Edgar Hoover and me together frequently, which made it possible for me to overlook my differences and softened the legacy of his hostile and unwarranted investigation.

As time passed, I found that my relationship with Hoover settled into professional perspective. I had first met him when he was fighting his early battles to build the FBI, much as we were then struggling to expand the Bureau of Prisons. I was aware that Sanford Bates resented the manner in which Hoover criticized the use of probation, paroles, and belittled prison people by referring to them as "cream-puff wardens." Hoover thought the solutions to the crime problem were tough prisons, long sentences, and less emphasis on probation and parole. Hoover appealed to the public imagination during the G-man era and became a national hero. In bureaucratic terms, he became "untouchable." One night when Attorney General Cummings wanted to get into his office after closing hours, the watchman refused to let him in, "even if you're J. Edgar in person."

During my years in charge of the Bureau of Prisons, I developed a considerable respect for Hoover as an administrator and builder of supporters, particularly on Capitol Hill. Though never close, personally, we were in day-to-day contact. He caught the criminals and I received them. Attorneys General Cummings, Jackson, Biddle, Clark, Brownell, and Rogers held staff conferences on various aspects of the crime situation and Hoover and I would always put our views forward emphatically.

There was a stock bit of humor around the Justice Department that the way for an attorney general to handle a crime problem was to ask J. Edgar about it, then Jim Bennett, and strike a middle course. While Hoover and I disagreed for the most part on our philosophies of law enforcement, we built up a mutual professional regard that survived the Petersburg incident. Hoover is a splendid organizer, a hard-driving and efficient administrator, a dedicated public servant, and a genius at overcoming the obstacles that perplex most government officials.

Shortly after the next change of presidential administration, I noticed that Hoover did not show up at the staff luncheons of Attorney General Robert F. Kennedy. He did not attend a single luncheon at which I was present throughout Kennedy's tour of office at the Justice Department. Hoover's prestige was such that he could attend or not attend attorney generals' luncheons, but I soon learned that Hoover was concerned about Kennedy's policies on crime control. Although I had been an admirer of President Kennedy since the days when his sister, Mrs. Sargent Shriver, helped us as a member of the Truman administration's Committee on Juvenile Delinquency, I found I was also watching Attorney General Kennedy's performance in office with disquiet. Kennedy's help in sending through my requests for presidential pardons for certain federal prisoners was invaluable, but his "war against organized crime" seemed to me to be politically rather than professionally inspired.

Attorney General Kennedy brought all these fears into focus when he told me, through one of his associates, that there was going to be a spectacular televised exposé of the grip of organized crime upon the vitals of American society. The Mafia was to be represented as one of the crucial forces in the country. Nothing was said about what would be done to the Mafia after its "image" had been exposed.

At any rate, I was asked to produce a federal prisoner known as Joe Valachi, a purported Mafia member serving a twenty-year sentence at Atlanta, for the televised hearings. I protested that it would be an affront to the dispassionate administration of justice to offer Valachi, or any other federal prisoner, as a public stool pigeon. I had on other occasions refused to permit the "bugging" of prison cells or visiting rooms, and I considered the exhibition of Valachi in similar vein. I expressed my conviction that the federal prisons ought to be objective, inviolate, and party to no deals. All the men had to feel sure that they were not to be "used" if they were to work for rehabilitation.

When I learned about the kind of deal with Valachi that was contemplated in return for his song about the Mafia, I disapproved even more strongly. Valachi was a typical narcotics racketeer who had been convicted several times for robbery, burglary, and extortion, with a record of arrests dating back to 1918. Many of these charges and convictions had been reversed for technical reasons, but he finally arrived in Atlanta in 1962. Not long afterward, Valachi left his work assignment in the tailor's shop, walked to a construction site, and picked up a piece of pipe. With this lethal instrument, he struck a prisoner named Saupp from behind, continuing to smash the man's head while he lay on the ground.

Valachi, apprehended at once, told the guards he thought he was attacking Joseph diPalermo, a Mafia agent who had been ordered to assassinate him. Valachi said he had simply struck first. We unearthed diPalermo, who denied the whole thing, and we were certain that Valachi killed Saupp in the course of a prison feud. His talk about his fear of other Italians in Atlanta —his claim that he had received the kiss of death from Mafia leader Vito Genovese—were clearly designed to divert the government agencies from the facts; he was building an alibi from the start. Valachi showed no remorse for killing a man who was obviously not a Mafia agent, and he was also badly scared. He knew he was guilty of a first-degree murder on a federal reservation and would probably be executed. So he wanted to make a deal.

At this point, the organized crime section of the Justice Department, apparently with Kennedy's approval, bit on Valachi's hook and swallowed it hook, line, and sinker. If Valachi would agree to tell all he knew about the Mafia on the television spectacular, the government would accept a plea of second-degree murder. Valachi consented to this arrangement and he was given a life sentence for the murder of Saupp. At the time, at the age of fifty-nine, he was already serving a twenty-year sentence that was almost tantamount to life. He got away with murder.

So Valachi was given careful coaching by Kennedy's staff and he appeared on television to tell his story about the Mafia and he filled the record with twice-told stories and rumors about the narcotics racket in New York. One phrase in his testimony stuck—"Cosa Nostra, "Our Thing," "Our Family"—and the Mafia image was established. Nothing that Valachi said on TV or privately added one iota to the knowledge of responsible law enforcement people about the Mafia. No one has ever been convicted on his testimony. In fact, he has made himself worthless as a witness and he has cost the government many thousands of dollars. His appearance before the McClellan Committee was little more than a publicity stunt. As for myself, I showed my disgust so openly that I was removed from any further participation in the affair. The responsibility for just this one federal prisoner was taken out of my hands and he was installed, finally, in the unused death house of the District of Columbia jail, where he was served special Italian dishes, plied with wine, given a television set, and permitted to talk to newspaper reporters. I was powerless to stop any of this.

Only after the Valachi affair was over were we able to express our sentiments in public. FBI Director Hoover went before the House Appropriations Subcommittee and said that Valachi's disclosures had no effect whatsoever in the FBI's campaign against organized crime. Then I testified that there had never, in my experience, been a case so lurid, so costly to the taxpayer—at least three hundred thousand dollars—and so devoid of result. Valachi was returned to the prison at Milan, Michigan, and the subcommittee chairman, Representative John J. Rooney, summed up: "Nothing developed from that nonsense."

The only side-effect was to create such a circus atmosphere about "Cosa Nostra" that Italian-American groups considered that they were being pilloried. When Valachi subsequently attempted to publish a book under his own byline in defiance of prison regulations, Representative Rooney charged that: "The book includes a lot of names which have already been mentioned and which belong to one particular race that has been maligned too often by too many people." Three years after the Valachi hearings, not a single prosecution has resulted from his testimony.

The Valachi affair was a case history of how prisons ought not to be run. It was a travesty that made a mockery of our vaunted protestations of respect for law and due process. It was, however, an exception to the good feelings that prevailed between the political and the professional elements of the Kennedy administration and the generally high level of law enforcement that prevailed during the Kennedy years. On the assassination of President Kennedy (to be followed not five years later by the assassination of his brother), I dispatched to every federal prison in the country this message about the fallen leader:

"President Kennedy was a man of grace, of courage and of charm who at the same time was a thoughtful co-worker who had become part of our lives. He understood the federal civil servant and his problems fully. While he did not demand perfection, he did ask for loyalty and diligence and for us, as federal civil servants, to sincerely seek to do what we can for our country. He knew, too, that genuine satisfaction flowed from that service.

"President Kennedy's life was a testimonial to his belief that a career on behalf of one's fellow-countrymen was to be preferred over all others. He could have spent his days in idle pleasure, because he was born to wealth, rather than undertake the anxiety-ridden, selfless and exhausting career he chose. He had the vigor, the vitality and the imagination to push forward projects and goals that others, more fainthearted, had considered Utopian. We shall not see his like again."

THE DEATH PENALTY

The mood and the temper of the people with regard to the treatment of crime and criminals is one of the unfailing tests of the civilization of any country.
Sir Winston Churchill

The grisly nature of the death penalty first became evident to me early in my career while I was leafing through a pile of papers on my desk in the Justice Department. Amid the housekeeping documents, I found a bill for five dollars, for the acid and cyanide used in the execution of a man named Arthur Ross Brown. How pointless it seemed. Brown was a kidnapper, rapist, and murderer. He had been put on trial on a Monday morning and on Wednesday the jury found him guilty, adding a recommendation that the death penalty be imposed. One month and a day later, we carried out the sentence in the gas chamber. Not even Brown's mother, loyal and loving to the last, would tease out a series of appeals she knew would be useless.

The whole sad business was handled quietly and expeditiously. Only one man protested, not against the execution, but against my decision not to allow him to photograph the proceedings in the gas chamber. The following morning, only a few paragraphs in the newspapers reported the event. If the point of the death penalty was to deter, I asked myself, who did the execution of Brown deter? Who even knew about it, and who cared?

Another morning I was visiting with Director Bates when his secretary slipped into the room and handed him an imposing looking document. "Mr. Bates," she said, "It's from the President and he's . . ." She stopped speaking and appeared almost to be holding her breath. Bates perused the paper swiftly. "Jim," he said, "the President has commuted Bernstein's sentence to life imprisonment." There was a silence. Charles Bernstein was due to be executed that day, in fact, in fifteen minutes' time.

Sanford Bates picked up the telephone and asked to be put through to the District of Columbia jail where the sentence was to be carried out. He hung over the phone, poised to speak the moment the call went through. "But, operator," he said suddenly, "you'll have to cut in." His face turned white and his fingers drummed on the desktop. The lines to the jail were all busy.

My mind ran over the complex details of the case. Bernstein was a young burglar and pickpocket who had served nine years in a state prison for allegedly stealing some bonds from a bank robber. The governor had pardoned him and set him free on grounds of innocence. Several years later Bernstein was "identified" as a man who had been seen committing a murder in Washington, according to the police. Whether or not he had actually been seen was a highly disputed point, but in any case he was a convenient fall guy with a prison record. He was arrested, convicted, and sentenced to death. Humanitarian agencies and government officials challenged the identification. The weather bureau clinched the issue when it said the foliage at that time of year was dense, and that Bernstein could not possibly have been seen through some trees as the alleged witness had claimed. President Roosevelt apparently had not seen the case until the very day of the execution although it had been under investigation and study for three years. At almost the last moment he had commuted the sentence to life imprisonment.

Bates cut into my thoughts. "The operator says she's sorry," he said, shoving the phone to me. "Jim, maybe you can get through. I'm going to tell Bill Hammack and we'll each grab a cab and run down to the jail. We don't have much time." I now had the responsibility for trying to save the life of a man at the other end of a telephone line that was busy.

I made a fresh phone call and told the operator to hurry. It was now ten to twelve, the appointed hour of the execution. "The line is still busy," she said. I told her: "Cut in now. A man's life is involved." Her voice came back as mechanically as only a telephone operator's can: "What is the nature of the emergency?"

I swore and told her: "This is the Department of Justice and in ten minutes a man is going to be executed. The President has just commuted his sentence. We've got to get through and stop the execution." She told me to hang on and she would do her best.

The operator cleared the lines and as soon as I heard a voice, I shouted, "Call off the execution. The President has commuted the sentence." The voice asked who was speaking. "Bennett—Department of Justice." The man said: "I'm just the officer on the desk. I'll connect you with the superintendent." There was more delay. Then: "I'm sorry, sir, but the superintendent seems to be tied up somewhere in the prison. I'll get one of the sergeants."

One, two, three, four, five more minutes ticked by. My hand

was tight on the receiver and the sweat ran down my wrist. The phone went dead. Surely we had not been cut off. Then another voice, a man identifying himself as a sergeant, asked what he could do for me. I shouted again, "Call off the execution," and identified myself. Another minute passed before the sergeant said genially, "We'll take care of it, sir. You can rest easy." Neither Bates's nor Hammack's cabs reached the jail before twelve. I had saved Bernstein's life.

Not long afterward, we were told through the underworld grapevine that Bernstein was a fall guy and that the murder had been committed by a small-time thug for pay. Roosevelt then commuted Bernstein's sentence to time served and set him free. President Truman subsequently pardoned him unconditionally. Bernstein went to work in a government job and dropped by to see me once in a while, though he had little to say.

How would we have felt if this man had been executed? How many others have died in similar miscarriages of justice we will never know. But we do know that Queen Elizabeth granted a pardon to Timothy Evans on the grounds of innocence fifteen years after he was executed. And dozens of pardons have been granted to condemned men on the ground their confessions were coerced or their conviction based on perjured testimony or mistaken identification.

Then there was the revolting execution of Anthony Chebatoris in the federal institution at Milan, Michigan. Chebatoris had been convicted of murder in a federal court after an attempted bank robbery in Michigan. The death penalty had been long outlawed in that state, but it was Chebatoris's luck that the circumstances of the robbery brought it under federal jurisdiction. Throughout his lengthy trial, he insisted he had not shot and killed a bystander, as charged, but that a police officer must have fired a stray round. Chebatoris was found guilty and condemned to be hanged.

Warden John Ryan of the Milan institution was given the job of carrying out the sentence. Reluctantly, he erected a gallows in the interior of the prison and surrounded it with a canvas screen. Then he located a man said to be an expert hangman. At two A.M. on the day of the execution, Ryan called me at home. "Is it all over?" I asked. Ryan replied, "I wish to God it was. The hangman arrived about an hour ago. He's gloriously drunk and he's got three friends with him, just as potted. We've given him enough coffee to sober him up a bit, but he says he isn't going to do the job unless we let his friends watch. He wants them to see what a 'pro' he is."

I reminded Ryan that nobody was permitted to attend the execution except official witnesses, but Ryan said, "I've been talking to him and he keeps threatening to pack up his stuff and get out if we don't let his friends in. They're all drunk. They can hardly walk." When I told Ryan he would have to carry out the execution himself in accordance with regulations if a hangman could not be found, he blew up at me: "No, sir, I'm against the whole business anyway. We haven't had a hanging here in the state in a hundred years and the whole institution's on edge. You and the attorney general can have this job right now."

We talked on some more, and eventually Ryan said he would go back to try to talk the hangman into executing Chebatoris. Somehow he realized that the hangman was too drunk to see whether his friends were in the darkened execution chamber or not. Ryan then told the hangman he would let the friends watch from the back of the room, whereupon the man agreed to execute Chebatoris. Afterward, another uproar began when the hangman asked his friends what they thought of the job, and they complained that the warden had kept them outside. The hangman promptly accused Ryan of trickery and deception, adding that he was not fit to run a federal institution. At this, Ryan's patience finally broke, and he threw the drunks out of the prison gate.

For obvious reasons, we decided to keep this episode a secret, announcing only that the execution had been carried out. There was something inherently disgusting about the death penalty that led to these excesses, I thought. Small wonder that prison wardens, not only John Ryan, but Lewis Lawes of Sing Sing, James Johnston of Alcatraz, and Clinton Duffy of San Quentin, were in the forefront of those who wanted to abolish capital punishment.

In 1935, while I was serving as an assistant director of the Bureau of Prisons, I decided to make up a list of the 184 executions that had taken place in the federal and state jurisdictions during the year. I noted that executions were being carried out at a rate of eighteen for every thousand homicides.

In 1964, the year in which I retired, I compiled a similar list. There were twenty-one executions, at a rate of three per thousand homicides.

Since then, the actual use of the death penalty has declined further. In 1965, sixty-seven men were condemned to death by the courts and sixty-two were reprieved. In 1966, only one man was executed in the whole country, and in 1967, there were two. In 1968, for the first year on record, there were no executions in the United States. Today more than four hundred condemned men wait in their death cells while their attorneys maneuver through the appellate processes. It is safe to say that most of them will be reprieved or their convictions set aside because they were denied a fair trial.

Despite this historical trend, however, the debate about the death penalty rages on. Of our fifty states, only thirteen have clearly repealed capital punishment. Delaware abolished the death penalty in 1958 but reinstated it in 1961. Colorado voted in a statewide referendum in 1966 to retain the death penalty. President Johnson's Commission on Law Enforcement reported: "Some members favor the abolition of capital punishment while others favor its retention." In this case, as in other sections of its report, the commission sidestepped the issue by declaring that capital punishment was a matter of policy for each state to decide for itself.

Overseas, there is almost as much contention. Great Britain suspended capital punishment in 1965, but only for a five-year trial. Most of the other countries of western Europe, and Japan, have abolished the death penalty unequivocally, while many of the underdeveloped countries maintain it. Canada held a parliamentary debate on the subject in 1965 and decided to retain capital punishment as a deterrent to murder.

Over the years, I found myself increasingly appalled by the nature of the penalty I was often responsible for carrying out. There was little question in my mind, as my experience increased, that the death penalty was revolting, susceptible to miscarriage of justice, and ineffective in the sense that it was not a deterrent to murder. I was affronted by the macabre methodology of capital punishment. I was shocked by the fact that men sentenced to death were generally penniless, friendless, and, disproportionately, Negroes. The death penalty also lent itself to erratic procedures in the courts. As Attorney General Robert H. Jackson put it: "When the penalty is death, appellate judges are tempted to strain the evidence and, in close cases, the law, in order to give doubtfully condemned men another chance."

On the other hand, I remain a convinced member of the majority of the public that wonders what other punishment may reasonably be imposed for such atrocious crimes as mass murder, the bombing of churches, schools, and aircraft in flight, and the assassination of the President. During my term in office, all of these occurred.

The heart of the argument in favor of the death penalty, of course, lies within Old Testament tradition. How can reverence for human life be protected if those who willfully take it are not themselves condemned? The death penalty is the cornerstone of ancient and medieval justice and, even as recently as the reigns of Henry VIII of England (seventy-two thousand executions) and Queen Elizabeth I (nineteen thousand executions), death was enacted in public spectacles intended to deter witnesses from breaking the law. One such episode, depicted by

Lytton Strachey, was the execution of three men, in 1594, for high treason against Good Queen Bess.

The three culprits, bound to hurdles, were dragged up Holborn, past one of the men's homes, to Tyburn Tree. There, before a crowd in festive spirits, one of the condemned attempted to make a last oration from the scaffold, but was shouted down. The mob howled with laughter when he asserted he loved his mistress more than Jesus Christ, and nothing more was heard until he was hurried to the gallows. There he was hanged and cut down while still living. He was thereupon castrated, disembowelled and quartered. The death sentence was carried out on the second man in like fashion.

But the third man, Tinoco, had seen what was to be his fate, twice repeated. His ears were filled with the shrieks and moans of his companions and his eyes with every detail of the contortions and the blood. Hanged, but cut down too soon, he recovered his feet. He was lusty and desperate and fell upon his executioners. The crowd was wild with excitement and cheered him on, breaking through the soldiers and forming a ring to watch the fight. But before long, the instincts of law and order reasserted themselves. Two stalwart men rushed forward to help the executioners. Tinoco was felled with a blow on the head and held down firmly. Then he too was castrated, disembowelled and quartered.

One hundred years afterward, the Earl of Ferrers was executed at Tyburn for the murder of his steward. This was the day, perhaps, in which capital punishment was in its blackest flower.

Dressed in the dove-colored embroidered coat and breeches that he had worn on his wedding day, the Earl rode to Tyburn in his own luxurious tandem, drawn by six gaily bedecked horses. Behind him in procession rode the sheriffs and other officials who had been designated to carry out the sentence. Next followed a coach bearing one or two high-ranking mourners and, at the end, a hearse drawn by six horses draped in the nobleman's black funeral regalia. At the gallows, the hangman and his assistant came forward and begged the Earl's forgiveness for what was about to be done. The Earl forgave them and, in an added gesture of generosity, drew five guineas from his pocket with apparent intent to reward the hangman.

But the Earl gave the five guineas to the hangman's assistant instead. The hangman promptly dropped him through the trap without any more ceremony and began to argue with the assistant about the five guineas. The assistant would not give up the money and, according to one observer, "an unseemly dispute arose between these unthinking wretches which the sheriff quickly silenced."

The modern United States was not incapable of putting on a capital punishment show, such as the shocking execution of Bonnie Brown Heady and Carl Austin Hall for the kidnapping and murder of young Bobby Greenlease. They were allowed to die together in the gas chamber, side by side, and they prepared for the execution as their last date. Bonnie Heady plucked her eyebrows, marcelled her hair and chose her shade of lipstick carefully. Meanwhile the question arose as to what she should be permitted to wear. Because a surfeit of clothing retains poison gas, it was first decided to let her wear only a bra and shorts and a pair of prison slippers, while Hall would wear shorts and slippers. Information obtained from the state of California indicated that gassed people could wear more, provided that the bodies were properly decontaminated. So Bonnie Heady was given a light green prison dress to wear over her underclothes, and Hall a gray prison suit. In the final hours, she wrote an endearing letter to Hall about the honeymoon they would enjoy in the hereafter, which Hall read impassively, and did not answer. When they entered the gas chamber together, he was stony-faced and indifferent, and she was as radiant as a middle-aged bride.

Although the execution was hideous, the cold-blooded

murder of ten-year-old Bobby Greenlease while his father was gathering the ransom was one of the atrocious crimes for which the death penalty might be retained. How else to punish the Greenlease kidnappers, or the men who blow up airliners, or Lee Harvey Oswald? How else to punish killers such as Carl Panzran, who boasted he had killed twenty-two people and vowed he would murder a prison guard to make it twenty-three. In Leavenworth, he accomplished his threat, and was executed.

Peering through the bars of a cell opposite Panzran's at Leavenworth was another murderer, Robert Stroud, the so-called Birdman of Alcatraz. He committed his first murder in Juneau, Alaska, at the age of nineteen, when he killed a man in an argument about how much money should be paid to a prostitute for whom he was working as a pimp. Sentenced to twelve years' imprisonment in the federal penitentiary at McNeil Island, he attacked and wounded another prisoner with a knife. He was given another six months and was transferred to Leavenworth. There Stroud attacked a prison officer in the presence of twelve hundred men in the dining hall at the Sunday midday meal. He pulled a double-edged dagger from inside his jacket and plunged it into the guard's heart because, he said later, the man had reported him for violating prison regulations. Stroud was tried and convicted three times of murder in the first degree, but the prosecution made so many errors in the presentation of the case that the first two trials were set aside by the court of appeals. Finally, Stroud was sentenced to death, but President Woodrow Wilson, in 1920, commuted the sentence to life imprisonment. Wilson's attorney general ordered that Stroud should be kept in solitary confinement so he would not be able to kill again.

One of the less formal aspects of imprisonment in those days was that men were sometimes allowed to keep pets in their cells. Stroud became interested in raising canaries and he was permitted to increase his flock. The Leavenworth officials even let him have a second cell in which he could set up a laboratory.

He repaid them for these privileges by smuggling out letters, defying the rules, and one day slugging the doctor who was treating him. Then they searched the cell thoroughly and found a lethal knife dug into the edge of his table in such a way that it could be quickly unsheathed and used on anyone who came near him. When Stroud's behavior continued to be recalcitrant he was transferred to Alcatraz, where he extended his studies and won his famous nickname, "Birdman of Alcatraz."

Under my administration, Stroud's case was repeatedly reviewed by attorneys general and parole boards, by members of the judiciary, and by our own classification committees, but none of us believed he was anything but a psychopathic killer. Attorney General Biddle wrote: "Stroud loves birds and hates men." Shortly before his death in our federal mental health institution at Springfield, Missouri, Stroud penned his own epitaph in the form of a dedication of one of his books on bird disease:

"To my friends and enemies, whose mean, little or thriving souls, actuated by spite, bigotry, jealousy, sadism, vindictiveness or ignorance, by their very opposition, have stimulated me to greater effort and accomplishment than would otherwise have been possible for me."

During the 1950's, I wrote a series of articles for legal and criminological journals in which I attempted to draw upon my experience to clarify my position on capital punishment. Now, as then, I hold to what might be termed the middle ground of the argument.

I am convinced that capital punishment is no deterrent to rape, kidnapping, armed robbery, or most homicides, and the five states with the lowest murder rates (Wisconsin, Minnesota, Iowa, North Dakota, Vermont) have in fact abolished the death penalty.

Another time-honored argument used by my colleague,

J. Edgar Hoover, is the one quoted by Sir Robert Grimstone in opposing the abandonment of the death penalty in England. He said: "No one can ever know how many people have refrained from murder because of the fear of being hanged." This sounds logical, but it does not hold when examined closely. All studies of the murder rate since 1920 have shown that the states which abolished the death penalty experienced no increase in willful killings; furthermore, their homicide rates are almost identical to those of contiguous states retaining capital punishment. A public policy of inducing fear of execution as a way to reduce the murder rate is a snare and a delusion.

Another tenuous argument is that to abolish the death penalty would indicate a softening approach to the control of crime and violence. Yet it has been made clear time and again by riots, police brutality, and unrestrained gunfire that violence begets violence. When a state is guilty of violence—as it is when it legalizes murder—it encourages the individual to be guilty of a violent act. That violence inevitably follows a war, or an execution, has been shown to be the case.

The courts are moving into the controversy. They have at last agreed that a person cannot be excluded from a jury because he is opposed to the death penalty. There are to be no more juries like the one described in Truman Capote's *In Cold Blood,* which was confronted with the question of the mental condition of one or both of the defendants. Soon I predict that our Supreme Court will decide whether the death penalty is "cruel and unusual punishment" of the kind forbidden by our Constitution. Surely, it is unusual, and it may be that in the light of present-day attitudes, morals, and value concepts surrounding the administration of justice, it is also cruel.

The least we can and should do is reduce the number of categories of crime for which the death penalty may be imposed, specifically ruling out the death penalty for most types of murder, armed robbery, and rape. As a concession, we may perhaps retain the death penalty for high treason, mass murder or multiple murders, the assassination of the President, murder for hire, the kidnapping and/or rape of children under fourteen years of age, and the murder of law enforcement officers engaged in the performance of their duties.

It would, I realize, be no easy job to draft a statute that would meet constitutional requirements of definiteness. What is mass murder, for instance, or how can you decide what is multiple murder? Is it killing two people, or must there be three or more as in the Speck case, in which a man killed six nurses? What standards should we apply to determining whether a kidnapping was actually the seizure of a person for ransom? In any event we must provide that before the death penalty can be imposed the jury must have full information about the convicted murderer or rapist including a psychiatric examination. They must also be permitted to hear the defendant at a separate trial devoted exclusively to hearing witnesses and the defendant as to the reasons for the crime, its motivation, and any and all mitigating information.

Even with this compromise, we should rewrite the death penalty statutes to provide that capital punishment may never be imposed by a single judge, acting alone, and that three-man panels of judges must be convened to pass on capital cases when the jury so recommends. It goes without saying that in capital cases the federal and state laws ought to be brought into harmony.

During my days of soul-searching on this issue, I was suddenly plunged into the most controversial double execution of the century. This was the electrocution of Julius and Ethel Rosenberg on charges of atomic espionage against the United States during World War II. I was responsible for carrying out the sentence of the courts and for months I tried to stave off the black day. Assuming, as I did, that the Rosenbergs were enemy agents who had transferred atomic secrets to the Soviet Union, I nonetheless doubted that the imposition of the death penalty was justified. I did not believe the country should be asked to pay the price of emotional confusion and division. I thought the Rosenbergs ought not to be placed on the national conscience or given the martyrdom they unswervingly sought.

Early in May 1953, I gave Attorney General Brownell a letter I had received from a woman. A passage in the letter read: "Americans are disposed to be just and merciful. I believe there must be many who may now have some qualms about the justice of destroying these two particular young people—among so many known agents, saboteurs and subversives—and surely some legal authority must know whether, in protesting their perfect innocence, they have lied or not. If they have not been reasonable in their answers to questions of known fact, they should be helped to release themselves from the bondage of a mistaken loyalty to a false cause. I believe that the American people would be greatly relieved in conscience if a true statement could be obtained from the Rosenbergs which would warrant their reprieve." Brownell was impressed and he authorized me to proceed on my own to see if I could persuade them to be more cooperative.

The strategy I determined upon, and discussed with Brownell, was to open a channel to the Rosenbergs that would enable them to speak directly with Brownell and through him to President Eisenhower. This channel would bypass the FBI, the U.S. attorney and the other agencies that the Rosenbergs had said they felt to be responsible for their arrest and "false" conviction, and might make it simpler for them to "release themselves from the bondage of a mistaken loyalty."

There was also a possibility that the case had become frozen. The Rosenbergs, arrested in the summer of 1950, had been sentenced to death by Federal Judge Irving Kaufman in May 1951, and their case had been before the Supreme Court seven times. If the Rosenbergs were indeed looking for a way out of their allegiance, I might be able to provide it. Brownell authorized me to interview Julius and Ethel Rosenberg in Sing Sing prison at once.

Three days later I reported on the interviews in this memorandum to Brownell:

On Tuesday, June 2, I interviewed Julius and Ethel Rosenberg in the death house at Sing Sing. I talked first with Julius Rosenberg in an interview room which was made available to me by the Warden. Following a short preliminary conversation about his health and the status of his case, I told Rosenberg that it was part of my official duty to arrange for any visits he might care to request with government officials familiar with the details of his case. I told him that there seemed to be a feeling on the part of some government agencies that he was in possession of information which would be helpful in solving some as yet unanswered questions. I stressed the importance of early disclosure of any such information he might have and giving government agents an opportunity to check on whatever statement he might make in view of the fact that the execution date was only two weeks away.

I had scarcely made known the purpose of my meeting when Rosenberg launched in a quite emotionally charged tirade to the effect that he and his wife were victims not only of a gross miscarriage of justice but a "deal" by the government on the one hand and his brother and sister-in-law, David and Ruth Greenglass, on the other. He asserted that Attorney General McGrath was the architect of the plot and had somehow influenced the selection of Judge Kaufman as the trial judge and was generally responsible for the outcome. He was very bitter also toward his sister-in-law, Ruth Greenglass, and laid great stress on the fact that she got off scot-free while his wife Ethel received the death sentence.

I questioned some of his statements and repeatedly told him that he ought somehow to be able to disabuse those familiar with the case of the feelings he had failed to make a full disclosure and had not been cooperative. Each time he protested his innocence. He also claimed that he was convicted on the basis of perjured testimony and trickery on the part of the prosecutor. He laid considerable stress on the fact that David Greenglass was supposed to have made the drawings involved from memory. He said it was impossible for a person of as little education and experience and knowledge of engineering as his brother-in-law David to do this. He said this in the course of his request that he and his wife be given another opportunity to appear in court so that all of the facts could be brought out. He somehow apparently believed that if he could have had another opportunity for public trial he could have vindicated himself.

This third part of his conversation consisted of a denunciation of Judge Kaufman and the sentence he gave. How, he asked, could it have been possible under any circumstances that a death sentence be meted out to him and his wife in the face of the sentence of thirty years given to Harry Gold and fifteen years to David Greenglass, who were admittedly arch-conspirators in an espionage plot. He contended that he was in no sense guilty of espionage and that the sentence was savage in the extreme.

Rosenberg lacked the detached calmness and self-assurance that characterized my former conversation with him. He no longer seemed to have the attitude of the martyr, which I felt marked his conversation the previous time I saw him. (This was a routine interview when the Rosenbergs were brought into federal custody; though held in a New York State penitentiary, the Rosenbergs were federal prisoners.)

Notwithstanding the fact that he told me several times that he understood I was not there to make any deal with him or put him on the rack, as he phrased it, he nevertheless was quite belligerent, excitable and made some statements that on questioning he was willing to modify. He talked much of Fascist tactics used in his case and inferred the sentence was not what one could expect of a great democracy, that he and his wife were of such small importance peoples abroad would never be able to understand our action in condemning them to death.

I next went to the women's cellblock where I saw Mrs. Rosenberg. I followed about the same approach in telling her that the purpose of my visit was to see how she was getting along and also to ascertain whether she wanted me to put her in touch with the proper government agents so that she could have an opportunity to make any statement or give any information about her case that would be helpful to the government in solving some unanswered questions relating to the whole matter. Evidently she and Julius had anticipated some such inquiry, because her attitude and her statements were substantially the same as those of her husband, although she wasn't quite as verbose or excited as he was. She said that obviously the government could not prove whatever suspicions they had about certain aspects of the case or we would not be turning to her for cooperation, and that she had no intention of putting her finger on somebody else or giving false or misleading information even though it might have the effect of staying her own execution. She said that if the government wanted her testimony on any matter she would have to be brought into open court.

Realizing that I wasn't getting anywhere, I asked the Warden to bring in Julius and to be present while I again repeated the purpose of my presence in the institution and told him that I would appreciate it if he would transmit promptly any message that either Julius or Ethel wished to have brought to the attention of the Department. Both Rosenbergs again protested that they would have no messages and no information and that the only thing I could do for them would be to present to the Attorney General a recommendation that their sentence be commuted. My final word to Julius was that I would be around the institution for an hour or so and that if he wished to see me again before I left to notify the guard. He said that he only wished to see me in the event I had some good news for him.

In the course of the interview Rosenberg asked me if I had consulted his attorney or advised him of my visit. When I told him I had not he requested me to do so, which I did later. I informed Mr. Bloch by telephone as soon as he could be reached, which was about 6 P.M., June 2, of my visit and my offer to expedite any request the Rosenbergs had bearing on a further explanation of the facts involved in their activities. Mr. Bloch expressed surprise that he had not been informed of the visit and invited to be present. I told him I was merely acting as intermediary and in my official capacity as the one to whom responsibility for their safe-keeping had been delegated. He made no further protest and merely said something to the effect that he would see the Rosenbergs the next day about some legal moves he had in mind.

After I had transmitted my memorandum to Brownell, I felt I had done all I could. He evidently deemed he had also done everything possible and I received no further instructions on the matter.

The evening of the execution, I joined the death watch in FBI Director Hoover's office. From the windows we watched the sad and bedraggled pickets parading up Pennsylvania Avenue to the White House. Some denounced President Eisenhower as a murderer. Others jeered the Rosenberg pickets as Communists and supporters of traitors who would soon burn. The police kept order while we waited beside an open phone line from Sing Sing, hoping to the end that the Rosenbergs would talk.

None of us said much, and I found myself mulling over the day's frantic efforts to locate the official executioner. In one of the customary, obscene snafus associated with capital punishment, the executioner had taken the day off and disappeared into the Catskill Mountains, telling nobody where he was going.

There had been another last-minute delay in the Supreme Court and the man did not expect to have to work that evening. Only by the purest chance did we find him in one of his favorite haunts in the Catskills and we brought him back by helicopter to Sing Sing. He arrived just in time to perform his task before the Jewish Sabbath began at sundown.

For two hours we waited in Hoover's office for word on the open line. The Rosenbergs had been told for the last time that, if they spoke out, they might get a stay. One of my assistants was on duty in the warden's office at Sing Sing to relay any breaks to Hoover and me. In the White House, President Eisenhower was on hand waiting to the end for any word from us. At 7:55 P.M., Daylight Saving Time, my assistant at Sing Sing informed me there would be no change, and the final seconds ticked away.

At 8:20 P.M., we were told it was all over, and we dispersed. Not until the following morning did I learn that the execution had been a rough one and that electrical currents had been passed through Mrs. Rosenberg for seven minutes until she was dead. Witnesses said a spiral of smoke went up from her head.

Into my office in the Bureau of Prisons a few days later two documents were brought special delivery. The first was the official record, signed by the U.S. marshal of the Southern District of New York, that the execution had been carried out. The second was a bill from Sing Sing:

Board, cell and special female guards for Ethel Rosenberg, 801 days $38.60 per day	$30,918.60
Board and cell for Julius Rosenberg, 736 days at $4.43 per day and 31 days at $38.60 per day	$3,399.98
Two executions at $150 each	$300.00

AS THE COURT PLEASES

"May it please the Court," said a young attorney assigned to represent one of the saddest men ever sent to prison, as he began his pleas to the federal judge for leniency. His client was guilty of forging the endorsement on a government check for $58.40. The man was thirty-two years old, unemployed, and his wife had just suffered a miscarriage. The attorney said deferentially that his client needed money for food and rent. He asked the judge to take into consideration that the man was a veteran, honorably discharged despite a light court-martial sentence for a single instance of misconduct, and had no other police record.

"This court," said the judge, shrugging his black robes higher, "intends to stop the stealing and forging of government checks. Fifteen years' imprisonment."

In the same year, 1960, another federal judge in the same circuit sentenced a thirty-six-year-old man for falsely endorsing a check for $35.20. This man was also unemployed and he had been honorably discharged from the Navy. He had been convicted of drunken driving, served thirty days, and he had spent an additional six months in prison for failure to provide for his wife and child. The court in this case felt that thirty days in jail was sufficient penalty for endorsing the $35.20 check.

While this wide disparity between sentences for virtually identical offenses was unusual, I noted over the years how often our courts pleased to be inconsistent. When I looked through the files of these two men, I tried to find some pattern in their previous lives that might have influenced the court, but found none. The only reason why one man received fifteen years and the other thirty days was that they appeared before different judges.

When Attorney General Robert H. Jackson was sent to the Supreme Court by President Roosevelt, I was both pleased and sorry. I knew he would make an able justice, but we would miss his earthy judgment of how well courts functioned, and what were the forces, circumstances, and prejudices that shaped their sentences. He once said:

"A criminal trial properly conducted is one of the best products of our law, provided you walk out of court before the sentence is given: if you stay to the end, you may find that it takes far less time and inquiry to settle a man's prospects in life than to find out whether he took a suitcase out of a parked car."

Jackson would elaborate the point by noting the protection that the law gives defendants regarding confessions, competent counsel, confrontation of witnesses, cross-examination, no self-incrimination, mental responsibility, due process, jury of peers, and the right of appeal on the issues of law all the way up to the Supreme Court. Yet sentences were often imposed in an off-the-cuff manner with no right of review.

Even though he had reservations about Mr. Justice Holmes's aphorism that "the law is not really logic, but experience," formed in the light of public opinion, Jackson would reminisce about a judge in his home town, Jamestown, New York, who framed sentences to suit the mood of the community. He would also quote a former lord chancellor of England on the attributes of judgeship: "First, the judge must be honest. Second, he must possess a reasonable amount of industry. Third, he must have courage. Fourth, he must be a gentleman. And then, if he has some knowledge of law, it would help."

Jackson always appeared to be searching for specific answers to the complex problems of sentencing. He would discuss with me the wisdom of taking sentencing out of the hands of the men in black robes, who acknowledged their own fallibility. He wondered whether respect for the courts would be greatly enhanced if the numbers game, as he put it, was removed from the judges' responsibility. The courts, he told me, cannot do exactly as they please. There are checks and balances as well as obstacles to be overcome. Most of our courts, particularly our lower courts, are simply not able to be more deliberate, to give more time and thought to sentencing, because they are swamped with work. And since Jackson's day, of course, we have been confronted with what might be termed a law explosion.

It is quite impossible, for example, for the District of Columbia Court of General Sessions to dispose of an annual caseload of fifteen hundred felonies, seventy-five hundred serious misdemeanors, thirty-eight thousand petty offenses and thirty-eight thousand traffic offenses on anything other than an assembly line basis.

Most of our cities have now adopted their own ways of administering "invisible justice" in which magistrates, prosecutors, and defense counsel settle everything out of court, and defendants are persuaded to plead guilty. This saves everyone the trouble of trials that develop the facts. I quote Dean Edward Barrett of the University of California Law School:

"Whenever the visitor looks at the system, he finds great numbers of defendants being processed by harassed and overworked officials. Police have more cases than they can investigate. Prosecutors walk into courtrooms to try simple cases as they take their initial looks at the files. Defense lawyers appear, having had no more than time for hasty conversations with their clients. Judges face long calendars and know there is no choice but to dispose of the cases. Suddenly, it becomes clear that for most defendants in the criminal process, there is scant regard for them as individuals. They are numbers on dockets, faceless ones, to be processed and sent on their ways."

Because these faceless numbers on dockets were often routinely processed and sent more or less automatically to prison, it soon became clear to me that prison reform would depend to a considerable degree on court reform. Accordingly, although the courts were not my bailiwick, I began to advise the many congressmen and lawyers who were looking for ways to modernize sentencing procedures. I compiled a list of injustices done to defendants in the courts and I was soon able to prove that our system was not so much cruel as chaotic. It even seemed that the courts were in a primitive phase of development.

I have mentioned the young mail robber at Alcatraz who received fifteen years on his first offense and an additional five years because he shouted at the trial judge. A bank robber in one of our prisons was given an additional ten years because, in an emotional outburst, he threatened the judge. An income tax evader appeared before a judge who had a passionate hatred of tax offenders and, to the astonishment of our whole law enforcement apparatus, the judge was able to aggregate sentences of an accumulated 177 months' imprisonment.

Not long ago, a defendant was sentenced to twenty years' imprisonment on a narcotics charge and, considering the sentence too severe, he appealed. The man was awarded a second trial. At the conclusion of this trial, he was sentenced to forty years' imprisonment (not now possible).

On the other hand, we had no alternative but to release to society a youth with a record of sex offenses and other acts of hostility who had been convicted of bank robbery and sentenced to only ninety-eight days' imprisonment. We also released a repeat offender, a burglar, who served his six-month sentence and left us vowing to steal as long as he lived. "Six months ain't nothing," he said.

I learned to discount the claims of the defenders of the system that these examples were isolated, relatively rare, and intended to discredit American institutions. These samples were not at all isolated or rare, and they reflected not only the vagaries of judges but also the piecemeal development of criminal codes.

The Oregon penal code contained 466 penalties that could be imposed for one or more of 1,413 offenses. Colorado prescribed that a dog stealer could get ten years, but a dog killer could get only six months. A first-degree murderer was eligible for parole when he had served ten years, while a second-degree murderer was not eligible until he had served fifteen years.

Under federal law, armed bank robbery is punishable by fine, by probation, or by any prison term up to twenty-five years, but armed robbery of a post office is punishable only by probation or a mandatory sentence of twenty-five years' imprisonment.

Actually, some judges go to great extremes to avoid the imposition of harsh mandatory sentences. Because a speeding offense, in one city, required the automatic and arbitrary loss of a driver's license, one good judge used to convict speeders of driving the wrong way on a one-way street even though there were no one-way streets in town. But some codes leave the courts such wide discretion that judges have little or no guidance and can impose extreme sentences if they do not like the defendant, or the defendant's counsel, or what the defendant did. No standards to guide judge or jury in determining what to take into account in imposing sentences are prescribed by law or court decision.

A jury in making a judgment on whether an armed robber, for instance, should be executed has unfettered discretion. It can hang him, it can let him go, or it can send him to prison for life without knowing whether he had a previous criminal record, was feeble-minded or mentally defective, or whether perhaps his wife was dying of cancer and he needed money for medicine to relieve her pain. A civil jury has instructions from the judge and guidelines for determining the amount of damages to be awarded. If these are excessive they may be set aside by the court, but not so in a criminal case. If a jury decides, for instance, that the way to stop armed robberies is to execute someone, they can prescribe the supreme penalty. And they sometimes do that, especially if the person robbing a filling station is armed and happens to be a Negro. No court can tell them no.

The courts dispense justice not only as they please but also to please the public that votes the judges into office or influences their selection. The third largest component of the crime index is auto theft, with 625,000 cars stolen in 1968. The judges of the state courts of Michigan, where cars are apparently taken for granted, let forty per cent of auto thieves go free in one year or less. But Florida state judges insist that eighty per cent of auto thieves be locked in prison more than one year, and thirty per cent are imprisoned for more than two years.

Another flagrant conflict in judicial philosophy surrounds the use of probation. The federal court in eastern Kentucky releases thirty-eight per cent of all defendants on probation while, across the hills, the southern district of West Virginia grants probation to seventy-eight per cent.

The federal courts have even more trouble making up their minds how to handle forgery and embezzlement. The average sentence for forgery in a recent year in the northern district of Mississippi was sixty-eight months, while in southern Mississippi it was seven months. Not long ago we received at Atlanta a middle-aged credit union treasurer with a sentence of 117 days for embezzling $24,000. He found there another embezzler of his own age, with an impeccable previous record and admirable family life, serving twenty years' imprisonment with five years of probation to follow.

Sometimes there is no pattern at all. In Texas in 1959 a strip-teaser was sentenced to fifteen years' imprisonment by a state judge for possession of marijuana. In 1962 three pharmaceutical company scientists who pleaded no contest to holding back and falsifying test data on a drug that allegedly hurt many hundreds of people were given suspended six-month sentences in a Washington, D.C., federal court.

Throughout my years in office, the appeals courts were crowded with cases that had little merit in terms of the difference between guilt and innocence. The appeals had been docketed not so much to upset the convictions as to overthrow unnecessarily harsh sentences. Appeals Court Judge George Edwards of Detroit estimates that forty to fifty per cent of his court's time is taken up by appeals that would not have been made if the sentences had been fair. Chief Judge Simon Sobeloff of the Fourth Circuit Court of Appeals says:

"These fantastic vagaries tear down the mightiest sanctions of the law—respect for the courts. In our country, we have good and wise men on the benches, but not all are wise and good, and even the best and most prudent, being human, like Homer, are sometimes inclined to nod. The truth is that passing sentence is too delicate and too powerful a function to lodge in any man's hands entirely unsupervised."

President Kennedy, whose compassion exceeded that of most men, struck out against the injustices that he perceived in our sentencing procedures. In his three years in office, Kennedy used his powers of granting executive clemency more often than any other President in our history. He reduced the sentences of more than one hundred prisoners and granted unconditional pardons to five hundred men who had been released and had demonstrated good citizenship. Without exception, Kennedy approved my recommendations for executive clemency and he invariably reminded me to let him know whenever I came across a glaring example of excessive sentencing. The President was particularly disturbed that a teenaged epileptic had been sentenced to life imprisonment on a narcotics charge, a teenaged boy to fifteen years for embezzlement, an Army officer to eighteen years for passing two bad checks, and he reduced the sentences to what he considered to be reasonable penalties.

Attorney General Robert F. Kennedy's contribution to evenhanded justice was also immense. He interceded in particular for a twenty-year-old man who lived in Los Angeles with his wife and children.

After acid was sprayed in the man's face in an industrial accident he became blind. His wife divorced him and took custody of the children saying she would not spend the rest of her life with a blind man. Soon thereafter the man recovered his eyesight. Desperate for money with which he hoped to win his wife and family back, he robbed a Georgia bank. He mailed the money to himself in California and, becoming remorseful, turned himself in to the FBI. His sentence was forty years even though he had never been in trouble before. Attorney General Kennedy, on one of his several visits to our institutions, heard of the case and recommended to his brother a reduction of sentence to fifteen years, a customary sentence for bank robbery.

Neither President Kennedy nor I believed, however, that the bold use of executive clemency was a substitute for sentencing reform. It was not hard to imagine how a diligent President, with an inquisitive attorney general, with computers in every courthouse, might feel tempted years hence to take over the administration of justice for himself. This was not the separation of powers intended by the Founding Fathers.

Fifteen of our states have recently recognized the principle of the right of review of sentences, but limit its application in theory or practice. My own state of Maryland now allows appeal against any sentence of more than two years' imprisonment. In Massachusetts, a three-man panel of judges may reduce sentences on appeal, but also may increase sentences appealed. In Connecticut, a similar three-man panel of judges had increased so many sentences that prisoners rarely apply. In Tennessee, sentences may be reviewed if imposed by a judge, but not if by a jury. In Oklahoma, the appeals court routinely reviews jury sentences.

No method of assessing sentences in noncapital cases is more grotesque than sentencing by jury. The jurors, as I have said, usually have no information about the defendant other than the basic facts of the crime and the testimony in court—no guidelines, no instructions, no standards prescribed by law. They know nothing of the defendant's prior record, mental condition, family background, or employment needs, and they are prone to be biased by the maudlin pleas of the defense counsel and the inflammatory statements of the prosecution. What juries often hand down—bizarre judgments—results in long and costly proceedings for everyone, with mistrials often declared. Jurors are not selected on the basis of their age, intelligence, sense of discrimination, ability to recognize the intricacies of a case, nor even the truth when they hear it. They are all too often swayed by considerations of race, creed, or their own image of justice as depicted on TV.

During the 1960's the need for real checks and balances within the sentencing structure became so apparent that a Senate judiciary subcommittee was convened to study the situation. Out of these meetings, the able and compassionate Senator Roman L. Hruska of Nebraska produced a bill that would provide for appellate review of sentences imposed in federal courts. This was the heart of the matter, and we were all delighted and encouraged when the Senate, in 1967, passed Hruska's bill. The House of Representatives has since pigeonholed the legislation, however, because the consensus of the members is that defendants are getting off too easily in the federal courts as it is. In recent years, the House of Representatives has become the arena in Washington in which cries for harsh maximum sentences and mandatory minimum sentences are heard the loudest.

Over the years, however, we did make considerable progress toward an integrated system of treatment of offenders in which the Bureau of Prisons was called upon to assist in determining sentences. I argued that if the object of the prison was to rehabilitate then our work ought to begin *before* the men were sentenced.

Our interest was to secure adequately long sentences for the men during which disciplinary, medical, psychiatric, vocational, academic, and social services could be brought to bear. We also wanted to assure adequately flexible sentences so that the men could be paroled without difficulty when they were ready, in our trained judgment, for release. Finally, we needed a mechanism whereby we could hold a prisoner after the expiration of his sentence if, in our opinion, he was still vicious, violent, and a potential threat to society.

Because I believe in an independent judiciary, I did not seek to infringe upon its prerogatives, but I did claim a voice in the disposition of offenders before they were sent to prison. The parole boards also hoped to be brought into cases from the earliest moment possible, and the concept of integrated treatment took on added scope.

In the years before I became prison director, there had been progress in broadening the power of the executive branch in the disposition of offenders. In 1910, Congress enacted a statute making federal prisoners eligible for parole after they had served one third of their sentences. In 1925, federal judges were permitted to put defendants on probation. In 1932, Congress took up the question of flexible sentences for youthful offenders and, six years later, passed the Federal Juvenile Delinquency Act extending to boys and girls of eighteen years of age or less the informal court procedures and the indeterminate commitments pioneered in several of the states. I drafted some follow-up legislation and found strong support from Attorney General Jackson, but we could not get these laws onto President Roosevelt's famous "must" list. Then World War II began, and the whole movement to reform sentencing was put on the shelf.

The man who got things rolling after the war was California's Governor Earl Warren. He persuaded his state legislature to approve the establishment of a Youth Authority, to which the courts would be able to commit juvenile offenders for an indeterminate period. Warren spurred on the construction of Youth Authority homes and devised academic, vocational, and recreational schedules. He pioneered a unique sentencing board to determine when youth offenders were ready for release, and inspired and funded plans for helping them in their communities.

Warren, whom I had known in the American Bar Association's section on criminal law, asked me for my views on the Youth Authority program. We also discussed a new kind of statute that would, in noncapital cases, relieve the judges of the responsibility of determining the exact length of sentences, and not long afterward California enacted it. A new Adult Authority was set up. The judges decided only whether men were to be sent to prison or placed on probation. Not until six months after the commitment of prisoners did the real sentencing procedure begin. During these months, the men underwent diagnostic testing by trained personnel and the caseworkers had time to gather personal information that cast light on the cases.

The Adult Authority reviewed this evidence, granted the men initial hearings, and set the dates on which they would be considered for parole. In effect, the Authority thereby set the minimum limit of sentences. On the parole date, the Authority measured the men's progress in prison and examined their "release plans"—home, employment, supervision required, and so on. Then the Authority decided whether to grant parole or not. The Adult Authority was also given the power to release men from parole.

The statute proved so beneficial that I thought of proposing an Adult Authority in the federal jurisdiction. In the meantime, I argued for a federal youth offender law and, in 1950, Congress approved the Youth Correction Act. Federal judges were enabled in their discretion to send youthful offenders to reformatories for indeterminate sentences or place them on probation. If they were unsure of what to do, or needed more information, they could remit the youngster to the Bureau of Prisons for diagnosis. I was authorized to make recommendations on the sentences and I soon believed we were making headway toward the kind of cooperation between the executive and judicial branches so necessary to crime prevention.

Specifically, the new federal laws provided for the commitment of offenders of twenty-six years or less to the custody of the U.S. Attorney General for a maximum period of six years, or for the maximum period prescribed for their offenses. They could be paroled at any time or held for not more than four years after their commitment. If the youngsters made a particularly good adjustment in our care and on parole, the board of parole was authorized to discharge them and set aside their original convictions. Thus we were given the power to clear men's records if we believed they merited it.

In order to implement the 1950 act, we designated our institution at Ashland, Kentucky, to accept youth commitments from east of the Mississippi and, two years later, our reformatory at Englewood, Colorado, was opened for young offenders from federal courts in the West. We redesigned and reorganized both places to provide for the young men on the lines of well-run schools, or so we hoped.

Whenever I floated trial balloons about an Adult Authority for the United States similar to California's, they were quickly shot down. This was, in part, because many federal judges feared any form of adult authority program as an encroachment upon their prerogatives and in part because they had misgivings about the ability of a federal system to handle the caseload. Congressmen of diverse opinions told me that a sentencing authority for all prisoners could not be enacted, but none other than President Eisenhower, who would soon appoint Warren as chief justice, directed me to keep on trying.

Attorney General Brownell and Assistant Attorney General Warren Olney, who was from California, finally convinced me that an Adult Authority would be unworkable in a system as broad, geographically, as the federal courts. They advised me to give up the frontal attack and instead to prepare several options that Congress could weigh in detail. I framed several test statutes and the outcome, several years later, was the passage of the Celler-Hennings Act, which many jurists have termed historic. The sponsors of this legislation were Representative Emanuel Celler of New York and Senator Thomas O. Hennings of Missouri.

The Celler-Hennings Act of 1958 was, in essence, an indeterminate sentencing procedure that the courts might use if it pleased them for most adult offenders under federal jurisdiction. Federal judges were also authorized to set the time for parole eligibility at any date before the expiration of one third of a sentence. If the judge sought more information about convicted men before passing final sentence, they were authorized to send them to the Bureau of Prisons for a three-to-six month period of observation and diagnosis. I was empowered to recommend the sentences that ought to be imposed and, on the basis of my reports, the judges could reaffirm the men's original sentences, reduce them, impose new sentences resting on other provisions of the law, or release the men on probation. This was a major gain.

The Celler-Hennings Act was close to much of what I had campaigned for, and my associates and I knew that our capacity for accurate judgment and sensible recommendations would now be on the line. In the fall of 1958 the judges dispatched the first men to the prisons for three to six months' diagnosis and, within two years, they were sending us thirty to thirty-five men each month. Within the prison system, I set up our own checks and balances. I required separate reports on every case from wardens, associate wardens, department heads, and caseworkers. Then at the bureau level we made up our own minds and reported to the federal judges. I was highly encouraged that the judges were soon accepting eight out of ten of our recommendations.

In another area of sentencing reform, I suggested that the federal judges might improve the quality of justice if they got to know one another better. I thought they should meet more often to discuss their cases and explain their reasoning and philosophy of sentencing. Out of this simple idea grew a proposal for formal "sentencing institutes," in which the federal judges in each circuit would meet to develop "a consensus of guiding principles for consistent and effective sentencing."

In 1959, the first sentencing institute was held in Boulder, Colorado, and it led to many others. Whenever my associates and I were invited to attend, we demonstrated examples and effects of unfair sentences and suggested criteria for judgment. We also acquainted the courts with the resources and limitations of our prisons and invited the judges to visit us. If it can be believed, only a dozen or so out of 250 federal judges had visited our prisons. Before I retired almost all the judges had made the trip. Sentencing institutes have been adopted in several states, and they are similarly effective.

Another major development was a system of "sentencing councils" pioneered by Chief Judge Theodore Levin of the U.S. District Court for eastern Michigan. This has since been utilized by federal courts in New York and Illinois, and by state courts in New York and California. In the federal sentencing councils in Michigan the chief probation officer calls a meeting once or twice each week to be attended by all judges with cases ready for sentencing. The chief probation officer and deputy probation officers are on hand. The objective is to review every trial judge's recommendation for sentence before it is imposed, and to subject that recommendation to sharp scrutiny. The procedure is for each judge to record his sentence and then for the trial judge to take the floor and argue for the sentence he wishes to impose. Then his fellow judges add their opinions, pro and con, followed by the probationary staff and the caseworkers who have examined the offenders' personal lives. The trial judge is not bound to accept the recommendations of his peers, but he is asked to reconsider if the panel so advises.

Levin says: "You can't expect uniform sentencing. That would be unrealistic. But what you can expect from justice is a uniform philosophy." By his tactful and persuasive manner Judge Levin has brought a brand of justice to his large court that is found in few other areas. The National Council on Crime and Delinquency has praised the sentencing councils as "the most useful of all methods" employed against unfair sentencing in the country.

On my retirement, however, it seemed to me that we had not been able to accomplish as much court reform as the times demanded. Justice Tom C. Clark, who has done much to promote practical, effective, and day-to-day administration of justice, once wrote: "Justice is everybody's business. It affects every man's fireside; it passes on his property, his reputation, his liberty, his life; yes, his all. We must therefore build our courts on solid ground, for if the judicial power fails, good government is at an end." Another Supreme Court Justice, Felix Frankfurter, put it a different way:

"What have we better than a blind guess that the criminal law in its present form does more harm than good? I do not stop to refer to the effect which it has on degrading prisoners and in plunging them further into crime, or to the question whether the fine or imprisonment do not fall more heavily on a criminal's wife and children than on himself. I have in mind more far-reaching questions: do we deal with criminals on proper principles?"

The vital issue here is how to select and retain able, independent, and incorruptible judges. An equally baffling problem is how to remove incompetent, disabled, or dishonest judges without resorting to the awkward impeachment process and without endangering judicial independence. Some feel that judges should be selected by the President or the governor and serve for life. Others think they should stand for election and serve short terms (two years) as in Texas, or long terms (fifteen years) as in New York and California. Others believe in merit plans of selection. There is in any event a general dissatisfaction with the present method of selecting judges once described thus by Attorney General Herbert Brownell: "All too often a judge gets his job as a reward for political loyalty, and looks on the courthouse as a cozy rest home." It is perhaps no exaggeration to say that, over the long haul, mediocrity in our courts is more corrosive than corruption.

Not long ago, I was elected a delegate to the Maryland Constitutional Convention, where we grappled with the problem and reached perhaps as good a solution as any for now. We agreed on a merit plan for judge selection that had been tested in Missouri. First, a judicial selection commission would be formed, with three, four or five lawyers appointed by the state bar association, and a like number of lay citizens appointed by the governor. This commission studies the qualifications of a large number of lawyers whose names have been submitted by the bar association and other civic groups, and sends a short list of three to five names to the governor. Within sixty days, the governor selects the new judge or judges from the short list, or delegates the choice to the chief judge of the state supreme court. The legislature then votes to confirm or deny. In the subsequent election the voters pass on the new judge not on the basis of party affiliation but on his record. They vote to decide whether he remains on the bench for a full term of eight to fifteen years by pulling the "yes" or "no" levers.

Under this Maryland plan, smaller commissions will also be formed to pass on the removal of undesirable judges, or to censure judges for improper conduct in office. And although the new idea is criticized in that it tends to substitute bar association politics for partisan politics, I think it represents a considerable advance.

The wonder is sometimes that we have done so well in selecting our judges by a system so dependent on superficial knowledge of a lawyer's "judicial temperament" and by hunch, generously larded with political considerations, also by the judicious cultivation of influential members of the bar associations. I came to know many of these able judges during my years in the prison service. I have admired their dedication and learning and I have valued the opportunity to work with some very learned and compassionate men. There were a few venal and corrupt judges, but relative to the thousands who occupy this high office and the stupendous issues and amounts that are often at stake, there have been amazingly few judicial derelictions. Only two judges served time in federal prisons in the twenty-seven years I was director.

One of the most outstanding men I knew was Judge John J. Parker of Greensboro, North Carolina, who set an example that often gave me the courage to carry on in difficult times. He was refused Senate confirmation for the U.S. Supreme Court after a campaign of calumny, misrepresentation, and prejudice almost without parallel. His nomination was submitted at a time when President Hoover was extremely unpopular, when millions were unemployed and the country was demoralized in the midst of the Great Depression. Judge Parker was challenged as a reactionary, a man far too conservative for the Court in those times, whereas the opposite was the case. Despite the injustice he had been done, Judge Parker went on to help us decisively in the preparation of a plan that promised justice to youth. This was the basic federal Youth Correction Act to which I have referred.

Judge Learned Hand was another who refused, as he said, "to ration justice." During the consideration of the Law Institute's Model Penal Code, which attempted to set guidelines for the whole nation, Judge Hand called attention time and again to the futility of trying to regulate what are called "immoral acts." He rebelled against using the courts to punish people for conduct they did not have the power to control, such as drug addiction, congenital homosexuality, alcoholism, and the like. One of his remarks with regard to sentencing particularly appealed to me. He said "Here I am, an old man in a long black nightgown, sitting up here making muffled noises at a man who may be no worse than I."

Judge William J. Campbell of Chicago is another compassionate man who achieves much. He helped me in many ways, such as how to maintain a balanced view regarding mental responsibility for crime. In my younger days, I was convinced that all of the law that had dealt with insanity and mental responsibility for crime was absurd, useless in application to particular cases, and responsible for horrendous distortions of our system of justice.

I pointed out to Judge Campbell that to ask a judge or jury to decide whether a man knew the difference between right and wrong was a moral issue that could not be determined by any objective person. The verdict would have to be based largely on the testimony of an overworked psychiatrist who might have based his judgment on how delirious or demented the man seemed to be. I argued that the better test was the one laid down by Judge David Bazelon of the District of Columbia, who wrote that a person cannot be convicted of a crime if his unlawful act was "the product of a mental disease or defect." In other words, if it could be shown after exhaustive examination that the accused lacked the capacity or the ability to resist committing the act with which he was charged then he could not be sent to prison. He would go to a mental institution instead. And in all due deference to those who administer our overcrowded and understaffed mental hospitals, these are little better as places of abode than many penal institutions.

Judge Campbell has now nearly convinced me that such rules

or definitions make little difference. He contends that juries pay little attention to nice distinctions or precise verbalizations and reach their conclusions on common-sense evaluations of the facts they are presented. They make their own decision on the facts and testimony without much regard for whether the accused really knew the difference between right and wrong or whether the act was the product of mental illness or defect. Judge Campbell thinks that psychiatrists only becloud the issue and should be kept out of the courtroom as much as possible. How we can utilize our growing knowledge of mental and emotional illnesses to prevent executing a man who may be deranged, or to keep a dangerous sex psychopath off the streets, remains a major interest of mine in retirement. Our knowledge of this whole field is limited indeed.

I am convinced that most judges are striving for more information and guidance, just as they are seeking to do justice by sentencing people in the light of their needs and the protection of the community. A judge must be a person of infinite patience coupled with a dispassionate recognition of the rights of the accused, as Judge Luther Youngdahl has said and exemplified. More important and more difficult to achieve is the requirement that bias, or desire to please any person, or win the approbation of the public or the press, be unswervingly put aside. These are the values that mark the stored up strength of a nation and test the caliber and extent of its civilization.

While there will always be fallible judges, we can reduce the possibility that justice will be delayed, arbitrary or venal. We must provide judges with assistance, advice, and information, so they may handle their high responsibilities intelligently. We must find ways of trimming the work load, and we must actively encourage discretion in sentencing. We must devise, and enact, merit selection and retention plans for judges if we really intend our courts to enact our inborn sense of fair play.

"Everywhere," Judge Josiah Quincy once said, "the robe of justice should be spotless; but, in that part, where it is destined to touch the ground, where, from its use, it must mix with the soil, there its texture should contain and preserve whatever there is of celestial quality in human life and conduct; there, if possible, its ermine should dazzle by exceeding whiteness; and be steeped, not only in the deep fountains of human learning, but be purified in those heavenly dews which descend alone from the source of divine and eternal justice."

XIII

THE NEW WAVE
OF PRISON REFORM

When, in 1960, I was appointed by President Eisenhower to
be chairman of the United States delegation to an International
Conference on Crime, I wondered what I might point to as
progress in penal reform in the United States. Had any really
new spirit, imagination, or experimentation been infused into
this ageless striving to stop crime through a system of imprisonment? Were prisons an anachronism? Did they, as pres-
ently organized and operated, have any future in a free society?

With these things in mind I hoped in the 1950's and 1960's to
be able to determine whether the traditional prisons of our
society, or most of them, could in my lifetime be done away
with. The Pennsylvania Quakers had proclaimed in 1787 that
"there must be no criminal class," and we would now try to
show that there was no essential difference between men in

prison and men on the outside. My associates and I intended to seek new ways of treating criminals as members of the community and, in time, we hoped to treat the community itself.

Our first move in this regard had been our development of the "prison without bars." This had begun, in President Hoover's day, almost by accident. In 1930 Sanford Bates was mulling over the fact that the federal system had not made much progress with its construction program and might not be able to accommodate all the prisoners. Bates felt the best solution was to take over a number of open work camps occupied by the Army during World War I but subsequently abandoned. The advantage of the work camps was that the men could be employed in useful and healthy activity clearing woods adjacent to public highways and repairing roads and bridges. But we would have little security and, in those days, before rehabilitation programs made their mark, many prisoners lived only to escape.

One day a group of leading Tucson, Arizona, businessmen brought us a proposal. They wanted to construct a scenic highway from their fast-growing city to the summit of Mt. Lemon and they suggested that the federal government take over the responsibility. The cost of building the highway over cliffs and canyons was too great for the city or the state to assume, so the motive of these good men was not altruistic, but they went on to give us the opportunity we had been seeking. They asked us if federal prisoners would be able to work on the project. We were offered living accommodations and a specific mission. In that rugged countryside it would also be very simple for prisoners to escape. But we decided to accept.

So the first open institution of the federal government was founded on a mountainside, eleven thousand feet above sea level, with forty carefully selected prisoners living in a few tents and a wooden administration hut. Work began on the scenic highway and the camp was expanded. Few attempted to escape. The project, in fact, turned out to be such a success that we were asked to stay on long after the road was completed.

Our men were given new jobs maintaining the highway, creating parks, clearing fire lanes, blazing trails, and building ski slopes. Selected groups of prisoners were sent far from camp without supervision to help the rangers fight forest fires. As our activities on Mt. Lemon expanded, the Tucson citizens supplied us with trucks, compressors, and power shovels and, in community educational courses, they taught our men construction techniques that might help after release.

Sanford Bates and I had less hesitation about proceeding with our original plan to start work camps on the World War I reservations. Soon, we had four open institutions with more than eight hundred prisoners engaged in useful work and, when I assumed the directorship, two thousand men were living in seven camps with the approval of nearby communities. This was now more than a test of a concept and I wondered whether, in restoring men to society, we really needed cells, walls, and bars for other than maximum-security-type prisoners. The way to handle the escape problem might well be the provision of incentives for self-improvement. Coincidentally, the New Deal years brought the establishment of the social security system, with its requirement of identification for most forms of work. It was becoming increasingly difficult for escaped men to stay long at liberty.

I was also anxious to move against the psychological problem of privacy. Within the massive penitentiaries, however humanely they were managed, it was impossible for the men to live even part of their lives in the privacy they might need to help them rebuild their self-respect.

The new idea was that prisons without bars would make possible the creation of a prison community. Once this was in working order and meriting local regard, it would be gradually integrated into the public community. In this new environment, prison officials and prisoners would be enabled to work together, to cooperate with the people living nearby, and to spread the meaning of rehabilitation for the general good.

Not until the end of World War II did I get the mandate—

and the budget—to proceed with the expansion of the work camps and to start our first prison without bars. In 1946, in Seagoville, a suburb of Dallas, our experimental wall-less, fence-less prison was opened for 450 men. The driveway curved between grass fields broken here and there by small trees, their branches tossing in the Texas wind. The main gate was open, and beyond it lay a college-like array of courtyards and brick buildings. Beside one courtyard was the administration build-ing and staff dormitory, and around another was an auditorium, school building, industrial workshop, and four long inmate "cottages." There were also two more cottages, an admission building, and a prison hospital.

Each of the inmate cottages at Seagoville was a comfortable, two-story brick building with sixty-eight single rooms. Prison-ers had their own rooms, 10 ft. 2 in. by 7 ft. 6 in., and the doors could only be locked by the prisoners from the inside. Every cottage contained two living rooms, assembly rooms, and en-closed porches in which families could visit the prisoners on holidays and weekends. The men and their families could also wander around the grounds.

We sent the most promising men we could find in the federal penitentiaries to Seagoville. We learned that most of the men in federal prisons in the 1950's could be regarded as promising. So we broadened the character of the Seagoville population, again on an experimental basis, until 200 of the 450 men there were serving sentences of five years imprisonment or more. We sent murderers, embezzlers, forgers, burglars, narcotics peddlers, car thieves, repeat offenders, first offenders, university graduates, and semi-literates to the new institution. The only common denominator was that these men had excellent chances for rehabilitation, in our judgment, and deserved the chance. And although there was some apprehension in Dallas that pris-oners would escape from Seagoville, only six or so attempted it each year and were swiftly brought back to custody. The penalty imposed on any man escaping from Seagoville was an increased sentence and transfer back to a penitentiary. This was a double deterrent.

Seagoville soon became something of a tourist showplace as its reputation in Dallas went up. A reporter from the *National Observer* wrote: "There is, in fact, a conspicuous sense of freedom and informality that continuously forces the visitor to revise his expectations of prison life. Several dozen men are strolling along footpaths around the area. Some are in small groups. Others are on their own. It is a mild day, and only a couple of the men have donned jackets over their military-style khaki shirts and trousers. You can see no uniformed prison officers."

Seagoville's rehabilitation courses began as soon as new prisoners were admitted. The men were interviewed and instructed about the purposes of an open institution, and were told they were responsible for their own progress. They would show they were learning from the retraining programs or they would have to be transferred to other institutions. Then the classification committee reviewed the case histories. The caseworkers set schedules of work and recreation. The men were shown the workshops, not unlike a small technical institute, with recreational facilities similar to those of a small two-year college.

In Seagoville, I decided after some soul-searching to introduce the kind of "student government" that had proven so controversial in the days of Thomas Mott Osborne at Sing Sing. Unlike Osborne, I was not a complete enthusiast about prisoner participation in prison management, if only because it could lead to undue power for inmate cliques, but I was aware that it enhanced the men's sense of responsibility. Since this was crucial to Seagoville's success, we went ahead, and "student government" worked very well.

One prisoner whose rebelliousness was changed, by Seagoville, from hostility, cynicism, and defiance to a completely new attitude of understanding, self-discipline, and cooperation, was Joe. His record as an auto thief with a reputation as a hellon-wheels driver and his resentment toward all authority did not really qualify him for Seagoville. But one of the correctional officers thought perhaps he would respond if he was convinced that someone believed he was worth salvaging.

So the classification committee transferred him to the prison without walls, guard towers, or armed guards. At first Joe resented the probing into his reasons for hating his alcoholic father, his inability to get along with any of his nine brothers and sisters, his aggressiveness when he drank too much, which each month before his arrest had occurred with growing frequency. He thought rehabilitation was bunk, the prison officers a bunch of bums who could not get a job anywhere else, and the parole board a lot of meatheads who released only those who should have been probated anyway, or had some political pull, or were "stoolies."

At first none of the officers to whom Joe was assigned could reach him. He "bucked" them in every way possible, "goofed off" and went to the hospital because of pains in his back, or so he said. But when Joe went directly to the warden and asked for help with the parole board, he was told that the only one who could help was Joe himself. He had to begin to "fly right" and show his resolve to change by going to Alcoholics Anonymous meetings, among other things. Joe's quarters officer, a no-nonsense former Navy chief, noticed him moping and persuaded him to talk about his troubles. Joe complained he had been given the run around with the "preachy" advice about the AAs. The quarters officer told Joe to "hit the road" for the AA meeting or things might get a lot worse.

So Joe went to the AAs and gradually, as he heard others talk about their problems, and what they intended to do, he began to change. Once he even made a brief speech himself. Also for the first time he noticed how the officers spoke more pleasantly and tried him out on more interesting jobs.

Joe's back stopped hurting about this time and he found he could do a real day's work in the shop and in school. He was encouraged by the reports the prison officers sent to the parole officer about how well he was doing. Finally came the day of another and different kind of interview with the parole board. This time he made it and a job was found for him in Dallas.

Ever since his final discharge, almost ten years ago, Joe has come back to Seagoville every month or six weeks to attend AA meetings. He is always the hit of the evening because, among other things, he can prove he is going straight and keeping on the wagon by passing around pictures of his tidy house and two boys.

More than a little extra money was spent on Joe, and some risky chances were taken, but Joe did not leave prison hating everyone and determined to square things by robbing a bank.

Seagoville's first warden, Reed Cozart, and those who followed him, set the tradition now espoused by Warden Henry J. Davis:

"We try here to create a climate in which it becomes possible for a man to change and, when you get down to it, to change himself. Under suitable guidance and controls, our men are learning that you can live more effectively by taking on day to day experiences and responsibilities. And, you know, that's what life is for most of us outside the prisons, too. If we do goof off, then it catches up on us some day, and we have to live with it. In the open institution, we give our men a chance to learn there is a better way. The words are 'self-discipline' and 'judgment.'

"And that's only part of the job. We have to look beyond prison. We must continually build bridges between the community inside and outside the prison. It is very tough to teach our kind of men that they can't be an island, that most of the time you get out of a community what you put in. But we have to try."

This was the spirit that actuated us as we sought to assess the lessons of Seagoville and apply them to the whole federal system. We now knew that many more prisoners would respond to Seagoville-type programs. We knew we did not need so many walls, bars, and cells and we could move safely toward less security in almost all prisons. With scarcely a murmur of criticism in Congress or from the public, I therefore undertook what appears in retrospect to be a drastic revamping of the concept of imprisonment.

Specifically, I decided to locate more than twenty-five per cent of federal prisoners in open institutions at once and to place another twenty-five to thirty-five per cent of the rest in minimum-security correctional institutions and reformatories. I also decided to qualify more than two thirds of the men convicted in federal courts, by the means of our classification procedures, for immediate dispatch to minimum-security institutions. The new arrival would no longer have to graduate from a penitentiary in order to reach a prison without bars. Finally, I extended many of the attributes of the open institution, such as unfettered visiting privileges, to good-conduct prisoners in Leavenworth, Atlanta, and McNeil Island.

Many of these reforms were suggested by Frank Loveland, who was the imaginative and broad-minded chief of our classification and training division. He was conscientiously and effectively helped by Gustave Moeller, his deputy, who saw to it that our ideas were implemented even when they were considered by some of our wardens to be visionary and impractical. These reforms pointed to new needs to integrate our open institutions within their communities, we thought, and this would require higher levels of skill among the personnel who would increasingly be in contact with the public. So, we inaugurated four new personnel programs.

We decided, for instance, to concentrate our custodial officers, caseworkers, and senior staff into "treatment teams" responsible for reporting on prisoners' progress. Previously, these categories of personnel had tended to form separate empires. The new system provided for constant and coordinated supervision from several vantage points. Each treatment team,

allotted as few prisoners as possible, was soon able to account
for prisoners at all times, and not only for classification committee meetings and parole hearings.

The treatment team system broadened understanding within
the prison service. The caseworkers, specialists in retraining and
in keeping in touch with men's families, had sometimes been
distrusted by prisoners and prison guards as disinterested snoopers. The custodial officers, though better liked by the prisoners
and similar to them in background and intelligence, had felt
they had little status and were looked down on by the caseworkers. But when the caseworkers and custodial officers met
together every day to work out their mission, they learned new
insights as well as skills. Not long after Warden John J. Galvin
brought treatment teams to the reformatory at El Reno, Oklahoma, for example, he reported that caseworkers were now
much closer to the men and that his guards considered the new
programs "the most exciting thing in prisons today."

The second and third new personnel programs extended this
concept. Senior casework aides were assigned to the admission
units of all federal prisons to guard against unwise work and
vocational assignments, and custodial officers were posted on a
routine basis for spells of duty in the casework offices in and
out of the prisons.

The fourth new personnel program was the introduction,
under my associate and successor, Myrl Alexander, for juveniles
at the National Training School for Boys in Washington, of a
"Cottage Life Intervention" system. Individual caseworkers
were made directly responsible for each cottage of seventy-five
boys and they helped set up group-therapy programs, under
the supervision of a group psychotherapist, a psychologist, and
their trained staffs. Although there was and is much to be said
against group therapy in the prisons, there can be no question
that for many of these boys it was a profound experience. "I
have to help myself with my problems" and "I'll get out of here
when my group thinks I've been helped" were typical phrases.

Group therapy has also proven effective in adult prisons in New York, New Jersey, California, and Utah, as well as in the federal system.

The National Training School for Boys soon showed improved staff morale as new ideas were enthusiastically advanced. I was delighted with one proposal that was reminiscent of the point system invented by Maconochie on Norfolk Island. A system known as CASE was set up in the training school in which the boys were given a fairly free choice on how they spent their time. They were awarded points for accomplishments, such as tests passed in school, work in the cafeteria, exemplary behavior, or excellent relations with the treatment teams. With these points, they were allowed to buy larger and tastier meals than others, to rent individual cubicles instead of dormitory space, to order items of personal comfort from mail-order catalogues. By the end of 1967, the boys were completing an average year of school work in five months.

These personnel and program innovations of the 1960's created an atmosphere among prison staffs to which many prisoners wholeheartedly responded. They also helped bring a new generation of able recruits to the public service and made it possible for us to embark on further steps of prison reform.

Work release was the name given to the next move to integrate prisons in the communities around them. This was an experimental technique in which we would actually release selected federal prisoners each day for all types of work outside the prison. The men would return to their quarters at night. Work release was a dramatic extension of the prison without bars, and it was advanced enthusiastically by Myrl Alexander, who had served as director of a prison worker training center at the University of Illinois. Alexander won the support of Attorney General Kennedy and of George Meany, president of the A.F.L.-C.I.O, once Meany was sure that the men on work release would not undermine the wages and working conditions of organized labor.

Work release projects were inaugurated at the Danbury, Milan, and Sandstone correctional institutions and at Seagoville. Warden Lawrence Carpenter of the reformatory at Texarkana won the hearty endorsement of the Junior Chamber of Commerce and found employment for all of the prisoners he recommended. This able and studious man proceeded cautiously, and thus avoided some of the mistakes made by overzealous state officials in Maryland and in North Carolina. These states sent long-term prisoners on work release who had served as little as fifteen per cent of their sentences and one out of ten attempted to escape. Our returns in the federal system were very much better. Because we first limited the work-release program to men who were due to be released within six months, there were virtually no attempts to escape.

The work-release program was important because we were putting prisoners back into the community before they had completed their terms and before they were eligible for parole. We were building up the men's self-confidence much as we had during the 1930's when we made our stand for Federal Prison Industries, Inc. We were also accustoming the communities around the prisons to the presence of our men in their midst. And although we had little difficulty in finding the first test jobs for work release, we were surprised to learn that the reputation of prisoners for unstinting work was soon such that employers were lining up at our doors and paying competitive wages.

So, we extended work release from experimental to routine status. Again from Seagoville, our laboratory, we sent out one in four of all prisoners, and back they came to the prison at night. Federal prisoners on work release were also permitted to save their earnings and send them home—an important factor in relieving financial pressure and restoring the morale of their families.

Nonetheless, the whole work-release idea barely survived disaster as a result of the troubles in North Carolina and Maryland. Following an exposé by the Baltimore *Sun* of assignment of an important confidence man and a banker, among a few other prisoners, to soft work-release jobs, I was asked by Governor Millard Tawes to investigate the newspaper charges. I found there had been no venality, no money paid for placing men on work release, but that extremely poor judgment had been used at the start of the program in selecting the candidates.

On the other hand, there were a number of spectacular individual successes that fully justified the work-release idea. One of these was Jim, a barely literate dwarf who stood four feet five inches in the high-heeled boots he prized. Because of his handicaps, he had great difficulty finding a job and even greater difficulty in keeping one. He was continually in and out of jail for petty thievery, cashing forged checks, and numbers peddling. But he begged the work-release officer for a chance and he was finally approved for placement in a woodworking concern whose foreman found great satisfaction in helping handicapped people.

Jim was tried out in various sections of the plant but could not hold his place in the production line. The foreman then built a platform for Jim to stand on and this enabled him to operate a machine of standard height. He was paid the going rate for the job and the money was sent home to his wife and family minus some institutional charges for board and keep.

Jim is one of many men who, if given this kind of wise and patient help, can be made into self-respecting, law-abiding workers rather than hopeless recidivists. The foreman is one of many employers who find rewarding opportunities to assist the disadvantaged even if they have been sent to prison.

The work-release program led logically to a further extension of the program—a study-release program. Initially intended only for youthful offenders, study release enabled boys to leave their reformatories to attend nearby schools and return to their quarters at night. Then it was decided to extend study-release privileges to adult prisoners at minimum-security correctional institutions. Model prisoners were permitted to attend night schools outside bars and bring themselves to high school diploma level. This experimental program soon proved to be so success-ful that it too was expanded. From the correctional institution at Danbury, more than seventy men, one in ten of the prison population, left the grounds every evening to attend night school. The results were good and there were few attempts to escape; those men who tried were quickly returned to close custody.

This was all fairly advanced prison reform in the 1960's, and I wondered when the counterattack would come, and from whom. I noticed one evening while watching a "CBS Reports" documentary on the prisons that several of the people in my living room in Bethesda were irritated that the prisoners were not "getting what they deserved." When the authorities at Danbury were shown providing transportation for men on work release, one of my guests said, "They're even getting free commutation." Although most people might still believe imprisonment should mean what it says, not a voice was raised in public to stop the new reforms.

One of the strange anomalies of public attitudes toward prisons is the fact that an overwhelming majority of people say they believe the prime purpose of prisons is to rehabilitate yet they refuse to pay for the teachers and the facilities required. A Harris Poll showed not long ago that eight out of ten people thought prisons should have constructive programs for re-directing their inmates, teaching them trades and skills and cor-recting their physical and mental handicaps. But when the same people were asked whether they would tax themselves a bit more to make this possible almost nine out of ten said "no." The budget authorities who passed upon our requests for appropria-tions reflected this attitude but work-release and study-release programs cost little to operate and they have been maintained and gradually expanded.

A system of furloughs for weekends, also to seek jobs and

interviews with possible employers, is being tested in several places. Such furloughs would help solve the pervasive problem of sex frustration without resorting to the Mississippi system of conjugal visits on the prison grounds. Similarly, furloughing of carefully selected prisoners, particularly youthful offenders, for home visits for Christmas or Thanksgiving, provides a valuable way of measuring their reliability and their potential readjustment to their communities.

This effort to develop neighborhood cooperation and integration of the prisons within the community also took the form of inviting as many private citizens as possible to visit us. I channeled these invitations at first to official and semi-official organizations, then to service groups such as the Lions, the Optimists, the Shriners, the Dale Carnegie people, and the Junior Chambers of Commerce.

So many people were soon coming to visit our prisons that we set up organized tours. Some of the best prisoners were trained in the history and purposes of their institution and they escorted groups of visitors around the premises, introducing them to other prisoners, showing off points of interest and escorting them to lunch in the cafeteria or staff dining rooms. For special events, such as the awards of diplomas to men who had completed academic or vocational courses, the men's relatives and friends were invited along with community leaders to sit with the prison staff and population at formal banquets.

This visiting program reached a high point one day in 1962 when 450 people toured the penitentiary at McNeil Island and more than 100 prisoners were assigned as escorts. It was a tribute to the Roman Catholic chaplain, Father Francis B. Prange, who had formed a large prisoner organization known as SIG (Self Improvement Group) and encouraged people from Seattle and Tacoma to join McNeil men in discussion groups on civic affairs. The big visit to McNeil was to celebrate SIG's fifth anniversary and I watched the proceedings with amazement. I was quoted in the local press: "Not a single incident has occurred that was in the least embarrassing. Five years ago, I would have thought that such a meeting could not have been even considered, but now I am convinced that it is helpful in bringing the inmates in contact with men and women on the outside."

The first pre-release guidance centers of the Bureau of Prisons were inaugurated in 1961 in New York, Chicago, and Los Angeles. We later opened three more centers in Detroit, Washington, D.C., and Kansas City. In each center we placed twenty men, all serving sentences of imprisonment and none eligible for parole. These 120 men were the pioneers of a program that sought to prove that prisoners could be treated within a community and that most prisons—even prisons without bars—were not necessary. This new concept was that the pre-release prisoners would complete their terms under careful supervision in the centers but would not formally be incarcerated. It was the most significant innovation of our reforms of the 1960's, and the state systems watched us carefully.

The New York pre-release guidance center was located in a neighborhood YMCA. The Chicago center took up twenty small rooms of a YMCA hotel with additional rooms for the staff. The Los Angeles center was a house. The initial intakes were youthful offenders who would be due for parole consideration within a few months. These were small beginnings, but the system prospered. Within months, with almost no escapes and none of the negative publicity that we had feared, we began to send adult offenders to the pre-release guidance centers. Then we experimented by sending youthful offenders there directly from the courts—i.e., we did not put them in prison at all.

New arrivals at the pre-release centers were confined for two days of orientation sessions with the staffs. They wore civilian clothes issued by the prison from which they had been transferred, or their own. They received visits from their families and friends. They were told they could use all the facilities of the YMCA and were issued free meal tickets for the YMCA cafeteria. They were welcome to join YMCA activities, outings, and clubs. Then the prisoners were grouped into caseloads by the staffs of the pre-release centers, with a ratio of one caseworker to every three men. They were given not jobs, but employment counsel, and utilizing this advice, they had to find their own jobs.

As soon as the men had established themselves at work, they were brought into a carefully planned schedule. They left the centers each morning and returned each evening at set hours, but never together. They were not permitted to meet during the day, being encouraged to make new friends and new contacts. At night, they discussed their experiences or went out again to attend school. Several evenings were devoted to sponsored activities, with attendance compulsory, such as lectures on "How to Buy a Car," "Social Diseases," "How to Budget Intelligently," and official films on "Why Vandalism?" and "How to Understand Others." Although the men were expected to account for their movements, in general, they were able to travel quite freely about the cities as they readjusted to normal lives.

As the center men began to accumulate earnings, they were required to meet their expenses, pay for their meals at the YMCA, and open joint savings accounts with their counselors. They were expected to save all their earnings in excess of thirty-five dollars per week for their first eight weeks in the center and forty-five dollars per week after that. Their savings accounts, rising into the hundreds of dollars as time passed, were a new experience and a source of prestige. One researcher noted: "In several cases the experience seems to have made them infatuated with saving, perhaps because it symbolizes a security and independence that most of them have not known before."

At points decided by the Bureau of Prisons, the pre-release prisoners were introduced to their future parole officers who, step by step, took over counseling responsibilities. At other points the men were told that they might eat at places other than the YMCAs, or sleep out with families and friends. The pre-release guidance center personnel were so close to the men that they were soon able to estimate who would respond and who would have to be returned to traditional prisons. During the first year of the centers, only 20 out of 174 men were returned, and the failure rate has declined since.

The pre-release guidance centers struck the public imagination. The newspapers coined a term that I liked tremendously —"halfway houses." The halfway houses were soon viewed as potential alternatives to imprisonment and, also, as a new type of institution altogether. The courts might eventually be able to send to halfway houses what they deem to be the "halfway cases"—the men not "good enough" for probation but not "bad enough" for imprisonment. The program was of course experimental, and our populations numbered hundreds, not thousands, but it was adopted by several states on the strength of our success. California, Michigan, Missouri, New York, and Kentucky opened halfway houses with excellent results.

The pre-release guidance centers have success stories to equal those of the work-release and study-release programs. One thirty-three-year-old confidence man, serving a two- to six-year sentence for larceny, had been arrested seven times and convicted four times for previous offenses, and his prognosis was discouraging. He was intelligent, of good family background, had been married and divorced twice, and moved from city to city. But toward the conclusion of his sentence, he was sent to a halfway house in Washington, D.C., in the hope that his release to the community might be phased, adjusted, and supervised. On arrival, he said he never wanted to return to prison because he did not want to live again with "those type of people."

This man at first stayed aloof from his fellow residents and the staff at the halfway house but, in individual and group counseling sessions, he appeared to gain insight into the mean-

inglessness of his former way of life. At any rate, he began to
work very hard at a lowly level as a counterman in a nearby
delicatessen and made one hundred dollars per week plus overtime. After three months he had accumulated net earnings after
paying his expenses of more than eight hundred dollars and
savings of about one hundred dollars. He began to take more of
an interest in his hobbies of painting and woodcarving. He also
met a girl who encouraged him to settle down.

On his release, he decided not to return to confidence activities but to continue working at the delicatessen. He was pro-
moted to assistant manager at a salary of $195 per week. He
married the girl, settled into an attractive apartment, and his
painting went so well he was asked to produce murals for some
of his new friends. His parole officers reported that his prognosis
for a happy and successful life was excellent.

Not so successful was the placement of a twenty-year-old
youth, serving one year and a day for auto theft, in the pre-
release guidance center in Chicago. His prior record showed
two juvenile charges, two arrests for public drunkenness, and
a second charge of auto theft that had not been prosecuted. His
background was a sad one: his father had been afflicted with
alcoholism and his mother had to raise him and his twelve
brothers essentially on her own. In his late teens he moved to
Chicago and entered into a common-law relationship with a
woman who was already pregnant by another man. In his work
as a short-order cook he was often intoxicated, and there was
confusion about a three-hundred-dollar loan he had taken out
from his employer shortly before the offense for which he was
arrested. But in the federal correctional institute he made an
excellent adjustment and he was sent to the pre-release guidance
center with high hopes.

At the halfway house, he was involved almost at once in two
drinking episodes, but he admitted he was inclined toward
alcoholism and expressed interest in Alcoholics Anonymous.
His counselor felt his basic trouble was that he had a low

opinion of himself. His former employer was interested in taking him back, but first the young man decided to obtain work elsewhere, and repay the loan of three hundred dollars. He got a job as a fry cook at $1.50 per hour, but was dismissed after five days when he became intoxicated and could not show up for work. The halfway house then helped him find work as a box maker at a candy company at $1.76 per hour. It was touch and go. Then one day it was discovered that he was responsible for the theft of four meal books worth ten dollars each from the halfway house itself, and that he had tried to sell them to other residents.

This was a misdemeanor and the young man was placed in the custody of the U.S. marshal and booked at a local police station. He pleaded he was sorry and "would we give him another chance?" The assistant U.S. attorney in charge of the case declined to prosecute and returned the young man for administrative handling by the Bureau of Prisons and the parole board. But there was no question that he had to be returned to a more secure institution. Parole was denied and this man served out his sentence in the old way.

A very interesting case occurred not long ago in Washington, D.C., when a twenty-two-year-old man received a mandatory fifteen-year sentence for assault with intent to commit robbery. Because he had no prior record, and because there was evidence of mild mental retardation, he was sent to a federal reformatory for an initial ninety-day period of study and observation. There his attitude and behavior were considered to be positive and diligent, and it was also learned he had been excessively dependent for psychological reasons on more criminal-minded associates. After three and a half months there, he was sent for an extended ninety days of observation and study in a pre-release guidance center in Washington.

He followed the regulations and the programs of the halfway house perfectly, and he re-established contact at weekends with his wife and three children, who were now living with his mother-in-law. Although previously an unskilled laborer, he was given a chance as a woodworker's apprentice, and he succeeded, winning salary increases from $1.60 to $1.90 per hour. Then, with the help of the U.S. Employment Service, he completed the Civil Service examination for maintenance and service workers. He passed, with an average rating. He budgeted his funds responsibly. All of this led to the question of whether he should be imprisoned or, instead, be placed on probation.

On the basis of his outstanding adjustment, the young man was sent back to federal court for re-sentencing. The judge directed that the fifteen-year sentence be suspended and that he be placed on probation for three years. His first move after his release was to decide to live by himself, work toward reconciliation with his family, and meanwhile contribute to their support.

The President's Commission on Law Enforcement, after reviewing all the evidence of success and failure that we could provide with regard to the new programs, concluded we were embarked upon one of the more hopeful campaigns of the war against crime.

The commission found that, "despite difficulties inherent in lack of experience in administering them, work-release programs have been highly successful." Study release, furloughs, and the halfway houses were also rated as successful and "particularly appropriate for juvenile and youthful offenders." The statistics of reduced recidivism helped confirm our success. The commission summed up:

"All of the new programs suggest that crime control can be increased by making the transition from confinement in a correctional institution to freedom in the community a gradual, closely supervised process. Graduated release permits offenders to cope with their many post-release problems in manageable steps, rather than trying to develop satisfactory home relationships, employment and leisure-time activity all at once upon release. It also permits our staff to initiate early and continuing assessment of progress under the actual stresses of life."

The final move was to see to it, in best bureaucratic style, that our new systems were battened down in federal law. This meant we needed congressional authorization for much of what we had accomplished. In this final mission, I knew that President Johnson would help us get the legislation. LBJ's drive in the White House was to educate, and it was primarily to educate federal prisoners to play their part in the Great Society that he submitted our statutes to Congress. In the years that followed my retirement in 1964, Congress enacted its own determination that in our country there be no criminal class.

In 1965 Congress passed the Prisoner Rehabilitation Act, authorizing the establishment of work release, study release, furloughs, and the pre-release guidance center "halfway houses." Congress also opened the Manpower Development and Training Act to federal and state prisoners, advancing funds to the states for new vocational training facilities and paying out allowances to help prisoners' families during their retraining. The Economic Opportunity Act was extended to enable local school systems to apply for federal funds for adult education courses to be operated inside the prisons and for courses on the outside that accepted prisoners. New ground appeared to be broken by the Vocational Rehabilitation Act, which set aside federal funds for use by the states for the retraining of federal or state prisoners "showing impaired ability to carry out normal relationships with family and community which may result from vocational, educational, social, environmental and other factors."

In 1965 Congress also enacted the Correctional Rehabilitation Study Act authorizing $2,100,000 in grants for a three-year study of prison manpower and prison service training programs. The federal funds, to be matched by private grants from foundations, were designed to increase the number of qualified people at work in all divisions of the prison system.

Last but not least, under LBJ's prod, my own U.S. Civil Service joined the prison reform movement. The Civil Service Commission had previously discouraged government agencies from offering jobs to former prisoners. Now the commission authorized part-time work for prisoners on work-release and pre-release programs, and full-time work for men and women on parole, or who had served out their terms.

PRISONS OF
THE SPACE AGE

*Man is a projector, a designer, a builder, a crafts-
man. His reward is not so much in the work as in its
making; not so much in the prize as in the race. We
may win when we lose, if we have done what we can;
for by so doing we have made real at least some part
of that finished product in whose fabrication we are
most concerned: ourselves.*

Judge Learned Hand

About two and a half years after I retired as federal prison
director, I went back to Alcatraz. I was ferried across the Bay
to the once-bristling fortress, still a federal enclave, in a fiber-
glass boat that would have fitted easily on the foredeck of the
heavy all-weather tender we used to ply between Fort Mason
and the Rock at least a dozen times a day. We were greeted on

the rotting dock by the caretaker's dog, Duke, part collie and part other breeds, who is supposed to bark the alarm whenever souvenir seekers try to get ashore. Why anybody would want a memento of Alcatraz baffles me, but there have always been those who collect hangman's ropes and torture instruments. Not long before, a group of San Francisco citizens had suggested that Alcatraz be turned into a monstrous waxworks museum in which the famous criminals—Capone, Machine Gun Kelly, Cretzer, and others—would be mummified in the cells they had occupied. Happily, the idea was turned down.

The gulls—*alcatraces* in Spanish—wheeled freely above the abandonded prison buildings as the last of the morning fog was blown out to sea. The waves broke over Little Alcatraz, the rock some fifty yards offshore from which we had once pulled a numbed escapee. The salt spray was splashing over the steel framework of a prison tower some forty yards from the Golden Gate side of the island, eroding the abutments much as it had weakened the steel bars and windows of the cellbocks. Responding to some nostalgic hunch, or bravado, or professional curiosity as to the extent of the erosion, I climbed out along a narrow pathway to the tower and up into the glass-enclosed housing where the guards had kept watch. The chair, for some reason, had not been removed, and I settled myself into it to admire the view.

I began to think about prisons, crime, and the law, and I wondered what kind of legacy my generation of prison administrators was leaving, whether in fact the groundwork had been laid for a new era of progress? What might the space age bring in terms of individualized discipline, care, and treatment of offenders?

As random thoughts occurred to me, a DC-8 roared across the bay. Why, I asked myself, had we not been able to focus the scientific energies that had perfected this aircraft on to the study of crimes. We were in the latter half of the twentieth century. Tens of thousands of federal, state, and local laws and ordinances had been computerized for instant reference. Data on scores of thousands of known lawbreakers, their character- istics and methods of operation could be printed out in minutes in hundreds of police stations nationwide. During my years in office, as the editorial in the *Atlantian* had said, we had managed to create a revolution in the prisons, but the gears of the penol- ogy machine still seemed to crash and rattle when asked to pro- duce anything like a "new breakthrough." To be sure, we now had some psychotherapy, tranquillizing drugs, brain scanners, and the like, but we still did not know how to change the behavior pattern of the psychopath, the homosexual, or even the obsessive-compulsive alcoholic or gambler.

Sanford Bates had perhaps put the challenge as well as anybody when he said crime was a disease or symptom of a social malady that could be treated. President Johnson organ- ized the line of attack when he tried to coordinate the police, the courts, and the prison bureau into his "national strategy." The objective was the rule of law—but none of these funda- mentals came to grips with the dilemma of the nature of the criminal.

Most American criminologists now hold there is no such animal as a born criminal, whose tendencies are inherited, in- evitable, and not responsive to reform. Each criminal is now regarded as an individual problem. His case must be carefully studied with reference to heredity, environment, personality, and known behavior. There is a general inclination to deny that criminals may be rigorously classified, except on the basis of such formal data as criminal record, repetitions of types of crime, seriousness of crimes, and so on. It appears that no uni- versal or single explanation of criminality is valid.

My own judgment would be similar, save for the fact that men with physical and mental defects frequently find it very difficult to make their way, to compete equally, in lawful pur- suits. They are handicapped in mind, body, or spirit to a point beyond the capacity of a penal institution to change very much, let alone correct. Some with obvious defects one can correct, as for instance the man with a harelip or a deformed hand or club foot. One of the more fruitful areas of research now under way in the federal prisons concerns plastic surgery: the way to rehabilitate a misshapen prisoner, so goes the concept, is not to spend years and dollars attempting to change his conduct pattern or scare him by punishment, but simply, instead, to operate to cure the defect.

I would never root criminality in mental disorder, because most mentally ill people do not commit crimes. Yet psychiatric treatments of all kinds have been proven effective in the federal prisons, although we have barely begun to tackle the problems. Small wonder, incidentally, because we have fewer than one hundred psychiatrists at work full-time in the prisons. What we badly need is a hospital for research in abnormal behavior, a place where we can send severely disturbed prisoners for study and treatment. Such a hospital was authorized on my recommendation but has never been built for a variety of reasons. The failure to follow through with this plan has been a bitter disappointment to me and a major setback to the government's protestations of leadership in discovering causes of crime.

The crime rate, as distinct from criminality, may of course be reduced by intelligent countermeasures that fall into every category imaginable. We have seen that severe punishment, up to and including the death penalty, does little to deter murder and many other violent crimes. But the threat of sizable fines and imprisonment has proven useful against other types of crime ranging from income tax fraud and official corruption to drunken driving and overtime parking. Great Britain recently cut down its traffic accident rate—something deemed virtually impossible in an urban society—by requiring breath analysis for motorists suspected of committing traffic violations while intoxicated. Indianapolis found that the simplest way to stop muggings was to light the streets more brightly. Auto theft would be reduced drastically if we insisted upon safer locks, stricter licensing of parking facilities, and comprehensive regulation of fly-by-night used-car dealers. Forgery and bad-check passing would be cut back if banks were required to conduct elementary credit investigations of persons opening checking accounts and if the government was made to print identification numbers on the millions of checks issued for social security, welfare, and veterans' benefits.

In the more direct sense, we need many more police officers, and they should be more highly trained and more highly paid than they are right now. There should be West Point-type academies to increase the sense of professionalism implicit in the slogan SUPPORT YOUR LOCAL POLICE.

The President could help make our correctional facilities more effective by emphasizing the age-old concern of the Quakers for humane, constructive, and just treatment of all prisoners. In doing this, he should make clear the vital role prisons must fulfill in preventing the unleashing annually of a hundred thousand crime-prone prisoners devoid of job skills, as well as in providing for their after care, supervision, and guidance.

In doing this, President Nixon should call attention to the fact that the funding of the Safe Streets Act of the Johnson Administration all but ignores the need for vast improvements in the staffing and modernization of the prison plant and program. The present act now sets aside only $1.50 per year per prisoner for upgrading our correctional programs—prisons, parole, probation, and juvenile training institutions. If the act is fully funded by an appropriation of three hundred million dollars, corrections would receive under limitations now written into the act not more than fifteen dollars annually per person incarcerated or under probation or parole supervision. The danger is not only that this pittance may be frittered away by local and inexpert groups on vague projects, but that it will also show that the punitive, starvation, "to-hell-with-them" approach is dominant.

Specifically, the limitations now in the Safe Streets Act should be removed and the executive branch given authority to allot funds where most needed or where some seed money would promise productive results. Also, there should be an act empowering the federal government to fund prison improvements, as it may now support hospital construction under the Hill-Burton Act.

The private sector should be encouraged by a system of tax credits to provide training and employment opportunities for prisoners and ex-prisoners. It must be remembered that at least fifty per cent of the hard-core unemployables have criminal or arrest records that all but completely incapacitate them for any but the most menial jobs. So they turn to dope peddling, policy rackets, pimping, and other forms of crime.

Interstate sharing of services in dealing with prisoners, probationers, and parolees is of equal importance to cooperation among the states in apprehending and convicting law violators. The callousness of "sunset" paroles, or probation on condition the prisoner leaves the state, or discrimination in treatment of nonresidents, is obvious. The development of interstate regional compacts for sharing of responsibilities in dealing with prisoners requiring specialized facilities and in the reintegration of prisoners in their home community is clearly needed. It must be remembered that, usually, at least one third of the men in most prisons, jails, and reformatories are nonresidents of the state in which they are imprisoned and will go to their home state when discharged. Some will be required to return home by the condition of their parole or probation. A bold approach to solving this problem may be made through interstate compacts, federal funding of transportation costs, and discouraging the adoption of cases by the federal authorities when cooperation between states cannot be secured.

Present statutes such as the National Education Act, the Vocational Training Act, the Juvenile Delinquency Act, the Safe Streets Act, Civil Service policies, and the like must be used to a greater extent to provide stimulus for recruitment of workers in the correctional field. They should offer incentives for training or transfer from one agency or state to another without loss of pension rights and fringe benefits. This might help offset the restiveness now occurring among correctional workers for recognition of their pay aspirations and drive for equality of status with the police.

Probation will continue to be scarcely disguised leniency until full-time trained officers are everywhere available, and every judge has a complete summary of the convicted person's background, criminal record, employment history, and so on before sentence is pronounced. A system of state payment to local courts that avoid commitments to state institutions has proven effective in California.

I would suggest also that in this space age we need a much more objective look at some of the time-honored, simplistic solutions to the crime crisis and I am not about to propound the all-too-familiar list of crime-fighting panaceas. *"Strengthening family life."* Is this an irrelevant goal in a society in which one third of all nonwhite fathers have deserted their families and divorce among white families is climbing to the level of one in three? *"Respect for law and order."* Is this also irrelevant, when landlord and tenant laws are loaded against the ghetto residents and almost anything can be fixed by those who know the right people? *"Cooperation with law enforcement agencies."* How many of our citizens believe the police push people around, and that the courts dole out soulless, assembly-line sentences? *"Harsher penalties and locking more people up."* Can these be solutions when all the evidence shows that coercion rarely works and that prisons seem to habituate their inmates to crime? *"Crack down on organized crime."* No argument—until this involves a crackdown on the numbers games, bookie joints, gambling, prostitution, and other pursuits so dear to our people. These are commodities or privileges our "good" people want. So long as they patronize the underground operators, so long will organized crime persist. Neither will I consider the current blathering against leniency by the courts. The most nonsensical aspect of life in this country today is the perverse drive of millions to lay down their constitutional rights to due process and privacy, which the courts are, quite properly, defending. Law and order, then justice, say the unthinking.

Unfashionable though it might be nowadays to question the late Dr. Martin Luther King, Jr., I must also draw attention to his statement that "Civil disobedience is a necessity sometimes. If there are unjust laws, it is our responsibility and duty to break them." His executive director, Andrew Young, translated this to mean—"We are coming to get our share and there is nothing Congress can do."

In view of all this stridency, what then, in the space age, will be the role of the prisons and the direction of prison reform? What will the prisons of 2000 A.D. be like? In her famous *The Crime of Punishment*, Margaret Wilson impressed a generation with her statement that prisons had not long been with us, and would soon be no more. It is much more likely, in my judgment, that the prison system will increasingly be valued, and used, as a laboratory and workshop of social change. Assuming, as we must, that the first phase of the treatment of offenders is apprehension by the police, that the second is disposition by the courts, then the third phase of treatment in the prisons will be the lengthiest and most sensitive. And it follows that, if we place the vicious racketeer to one side of the spectrum, and the compulsive petty offender on the other, we are left with the vast majority of our criminal population. Individualized discipline, care, and treatment of these people will be wholly possible.

The prisons of the space age will be small—federal, state, and local—with populations of no more than six hundred men. They will be specialized to a degree not even envisaged today. They will be equipped to serve as diagnostic centers to advise the courts on sentencing—and this might well become standard operating procedure. Because it will pay, correctional facilities will be able to program and manage rehabilitation schedules for each individual prisoner almost on a tutorial basis. They will organize work for every man, in and out of the institution, on the same individual basis.

The point of the prisons of the space age is that they will enlist the resources of the communities in the treatment of their own wrongdoers. The prisons will be shaped to suit regional population groupings, and will have means to assist the misdemeanant as well as treat the handicapped and the mentally disturbed. These all-purpose correctional institutions will be managed by career personnel selected on a merit basis, overseen by committees of leading citizens, part elected, part appointed. There will be a very clear call within the community—in time, it might even amount to a requirement and perhaps it should be—for volunteer work inside the prisons. The operating costs of the small space-age prisons will be prorated among the communities served, and federal and state contributions will also be allotted on a prorate basis.

These new, modern, open prisons will of course bear no resemblance to the penitentiaries of today. There will be no more San Quentins, Sing Sings, Leavenworths, and Atlantas. There will be no more mammoth fortified bastilles, and few watchtowers, searchlights, and, perhaps, not even bells. There will be several small maximum-security prisons in both the federal and state jurisdictions where the desperate criminals will be kept safely fenced away from society. But the new emphasis will be decentralization.

There will have long since been a new definition of offenses: surely we will, any year now, remove the drug addicts, alcoholics, sex deviants and mental defectives from our overcrowded correctional process. Surely we will soon confine them in clinics for cure, rather than lock them in prisons for punishment. There has been notable progress everywhere in the country in this regard. The courts might soon decide the matter by finding it is "cruel and unusual punishment" to incarcerate sick people, and therefore unconstitutional.

Yet decentralization can never be all-pervasive: the federal prisons, also small, will endeavor to set examples and standards of humane discipline and advanced rehabilitation, will meet critical shortages and assume special responsibilities for the more difficult prisoners the several regions may not be able to handle. Because it is rooted in human nature, cruelty within the prisons will always be a problem: enforceable methods will have to be found to ensure that the small prisons within the communities measure up to nationwide standards of treating people in custody, or face financial and legal penalties. The federal government will have ample leverage in its money powers, and in this respect decentralization will be subordinate to considerations of humane treatment. When President Johnson requested federal appropriations to aid the states in their campaigns against crime, he said: "Crime is no longer merely a local problem. Every city, every state is troubled by the same, hard statistical facts. The extent and seriousness of the problem have made it a great national concern."

So the new prisons, even as they are adapted more skillfully to serve the needs of the communities, will yet be guided in the interests of the area as a whole. These important goals can be achieved through the development of interstate compacts or regional organizations, much as we deal with air pollution, clean water problems, and regional transportation.

While I contemplated these achievable goals from my glass and steel tower at Alcatraz above the waters of the Golden Gate, I wondered briefly whether my youthful decision to choose prison, to pursue the rule of law, had been a grave miscalculation. Was there not some other area of social activity in which my time might have been better spent? After all, the focus was now to be war against poverty, an eradication of the slums, an advance of education, a swelling cry for brotherhood, and perhaps there might have been more fertile fields than prison reform. Yet when I thought back across the saga from Beccaria to today—when I looked down on our dead maximum-security prison as a symbol of how far we had come—I knew I had not wasted my time. Others had gone before and others would follow.

On that note of solace, I started down from the tower and, as I did so, I knew why I had so devoted my time. My motive was and will be never that of a visionary or radical changer of lives or laws, but solely of a man who hates intolerance, injustice, and defeatism.

I believe there is a treasure in the heart of every man if we can find it—*if we can help him find it.*

I believe this is the true way to fight crime.

INDEX

A NOTE ABOUT THE AUTHOR

James V. Bennett was born in Silver Creek, New York, in 1894, the son of an Episcopal clergyman. He was educated at Brown University and George Washington University, where he received an LL.B. in 1926. After serving in the Army around the end of World War I, Mr. Bennett became an investigator for the Bureau of Efficiency. In 1930 he was made an assistant director of the U.S. Bureau of Prisons. He was appointed director of the prison bureau in 1937 by President Roosevelt and reappointed by Presidents Truman, Eisenhower, and Kennedy, until his retirement in 1964. Since that time he has continued his activities in prison reform and become a leader in the movement for firearms control.

NOTE ABOUT THE EDITOR

Rodney C. Campbell, formerly a foreign correspondent for the London Sunday Times, *associate editor of* Time *Magazine, and editor of* USA*1 *Magazine, is now an editorial adviser to publishing, industrial, and advertising organizations and an editorial consultant to Governor Nelson A. Rockefeller of New York.*

A NOTE ON THE TYPE

The text of this book was set on the Linotype in Janson, a recutting made direct from type cast from matrices long thought to have been made by the Dutchman Anton Janson, who was a practicing type founder in Leipzig during the years 1868–78. However, it has been conclusively demonstrated that these types are actually the work of Nicholas Kis (1650–1702), a Hungarian, who most probably learned his trade from the master Dutch type founder Kirk Voskens. The type is an excellent example of the influential and sturdy Dutch types that prevailed in England up to the time William Caslon developed his own incomparable designs from these Dutch faces.

The book was composed, printed and bound by The Book Press, Brattleboro, Vermont. Typography and binding design by Barbara Haner.